YOUR
DIET
COACH

YOUR DIET COACH

Barbara DeBetz, M.D.

Produced by The Philip Lief Group, Inc.

PRENTICE
HALL
PRESS

NEW YORK   LONDON   TORONTO   SYDNEY   TOKYO

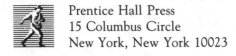 Prentice Hall Press
15 Columbus Circle
New York, New York 10023

Copyright © 1989 by Barbara DeBetz, M.D.
Produced by The Philip Lief Group, Inc.

Library of Congress Cataloging-in-Publication Data

DeBetz, Barbara.
    Your diet coach/Barbara DeBetz—1st Prentice Hall Press ed.
      p. cm.
    "Produced by the Philip Lief Group, Inc."
    ISBN 0-13-761966-9: $10.95
    1. Reducing—Psychological aspects.   2. Motivation (Psychology)
I. Title.
RM222.D42   1989
613.2′5—dc20   89-16342
                                                         CIP

Designed by Robert Bull Design

Manufactured in the U.S.A.

10 9 8 7 6 5 4 3 2 1

First Edition

For my sister Ingrid,
a never-ending source of love, support, and encouragement.

Acknowledgments

A special thanks to Cathy Hemming and Jamie Rothstein of the Philip Lief Group, and to Marilyn Abraham of Prentice Hall Press, for their enthusiasm and encouragement.

I would especially like to thank Susan Waggoner, whose creative input was a valuable contribution to this book.

CONTENTS

INTRODUCTION

AS A psychiatrist specializing in weight control, I have helped hundreds of people shed unwanted pounds. Many of them have been heavy all their lives—and many of them haven't. Many have dieted before—and many haven't. Many of them have discovered they eat for psychological reasons—and many have discovered they eat simply because food tastes good.

Despite the picture that has often been painted of the overweight person as neurotic, lacking in willpower, and destined to be fat, this simply isn't true. There is no "representative" overweight person, and losing weight is more than just a matter of taking in fewer calories.

Why is it, then, that some people can lose weight and keep it off while others try again and again without success? The answer comes in a single word: *motivation.*

Let's take a moment to do a quick self-test. What's your motivation level right now? Is it high? Low? Medium? Nonexistent? Draw a line on the bar graph on the following page to indicate where your motivation is.

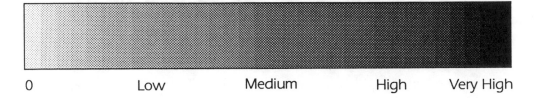

| 0 | Low | Medium | High | Very High |

I hope you didn't draw a line at 0! The very fact that you picked up this book is proof that you have some degree of motivation. Today, for whatever reason, you want to lose weight badly enough to do something about it.

"But what if my motivation isn't *enough?*" patients often ask.

Most people think that motivation is a fixed quantity, something you either have or haven't got. Many diet programs work on the same premise, taking it for granted that you're "psyched up" and can keep yourself that way.

This kind of thinking is a mistake—a mistake this book will teach you how to correct. The truth is that motivation is not a fixed or finite thing. It's something that can—and must—be constantly nourished and strengthened. Even a small amount of motivation can be fanned into a bonfire if it is properly cared for. And, conversely, a high amount of motivation can die out if it isn't replenished.

Your Diet Coach will show you how to get the most out of your motivation. You'll learn how to reinforce it and keep it going strong through each and every day of your diet.

The unique program revealed in this book allows you to take control of your mind as well as your body. If you follow it you will do more than just lose weight. You will free yourself from the mental anguish so many people experience when trying to diet: the cravings that you don't know how to deal with, the recriminations over debilitating failures, the fear that you are not and never will be in charge.

This program will teach you how to take control of your eating and maintain that control for the rest of your life. The program does not involve any of the platitudes or slogans you have heard before. Simply telling someone to "think thin" is like asking her to do a one-and-a-half gainer off the high board before they've put a toe in the water.

Nor does the program involve an endless series of *don'ts*. Many people who put on extra weight are achievers by nature. They are very efficient at getting things done, a trait that they have carried to the dinner table. If you have been eating too much, food has come to occupy a large place in your life. It has filled time and directed your activities. Perhaps it has even been the focus of your social life. When you give up overeating, the empty spaces aren't just in your stomach.

This book will show you how to fill your empty spaces by teaching you how to redirect your activities, your thoughts, and your beliefs about food. What it will offer you are specific, action-oriented techniques to employ whenever you feel your motivation weakening. You can employ these techniques anytime, anywhere. Best of all, they are so simple that you will never forget them. You will be able to use them for the rest of your life. *You will never have to feel out of control again.*

To accomplish this miracle, only one thing is needed: your complete cooperation.

If you were to come to my office, we would spend a great deal of time together, sometimes just the two of us, sometimes in a group situation. As we talked, you would discover truths about yourself that previously seemed hidden. Such new awarenesses, coupled with the techniques in my program, will be your tools for success.

This book has been carefully designed with you in mind. It is not really a "diet" book but an interactive program. It will allow you to see your own problem clearly, and to devise strategies that will work for you. No more accepting diets and diagnoses that don't fit. No more looking outside yourself for motivation.

How to Use This Book

Now, as you are reading this, take a moment to leaf through the book. You will see that it is arranged into ten separate days. I want you to move through the book one day at a time, working through the exercises each day and acquiring the tools presented. Each day has been carefully planned to build your motivation over this period of time. To make the book work for you, you will need to set your "Take-Off Day"—the day you will begin your diet. Then, working backwards, begin reading ten days before you begin your diet. As you *count down* to Take-Off Day, you will also *build up* your motivation and add to the arsenal of tools and strategies that will allow you to diet successfully.

As you page through this book, you will also notice that there are plenty of blank spaces. These have not been included to make the book look nice or to boost the profits of the paper industry. They have been put there for you to use. Ten days from now, the day you begin to diet (Take-Off Day), those blank spaces should be filled in.

Do not simply think about filling them in—*do it!* Thoughts can be elusive. They can slip through your fingers in ways spoken and written words cannot. In my practice, I have seen over and over again the power of spoken and written words. How often they have served as stepping-stones to deeper awarenesses and new levels of commitment! Each time you fill in a blank, respond to a question, or jot down an awareness, you are identifying and breaking free of your destructive eating patterns. You are strengthening your motivation and moving one step closer to your goal.

Just to see how painless this process will be, let's practice.

A few minutes ago I told you that your cooperation would be needed to make this program succeed. Cooperation, in this case, means writing down answers and observations throughout this book. Are you willing to do that?

(Your answer) _____

See how easy that was?

Other exercises you will be asked to do will take more time, and some of them may be more difficult for you. But don't worry that you won't make it—you will. You will not be asked to do anything you are not capable of doing, or to take any steps that hundreds of others have not taken before you. The journey you think of as difficult and perhaps even impossible is not impossible at all. In fact, the journey has already begun. You took the first step when you picked up this book. You took another when you began reading this brief introduction and yet another when you answered the question above. Now all you have to do is let the momentum of your own motivation—reinforced by the techniques you will learn from this book—carry you to your goal!

MOTIVATION 101
A SHORT COURSE

PAT: I *should* be motivated.

HENRY: When I'm around food, I just lose my motivation to diet.

IKE: I have plenty of motivation when it comes to my career, but when it comes to controlling my diet—forget it!

JOANNE: Dr. DeBetz, can you give me some motivation?

THESE STATEMENTS are typical of conversations that go on in my office every day. Look at them again and at the negative, self-defeating words linked to the magic word *motivation*.

Pat puts herself down by saying that she *should* be motivated. Henry believes that food is an all-powerful substance that causes him to lose his motivation. Ike waves the white flag of surrender by conceding that when it comes to eating, he doesn't have any motivation at all. And Joanne reduces her status to that of a beggar who must ask to be *given* her motivation.

What do all of these people have in common? They see themselves as doomed to dieting failure because they don't possess sufficient amounts of that mercurial quality *motivation*.

Is this how you feel about yourself, too? If it is, then this book is going to make a very big difference in your life. A difference that will allow you to take control of your eating. A difference that will allow you to achieve and maintain—perhaps for the first time in your life—a slim and healthy weight.

Do you have a pencil handy? If you don't, go get one. Get into the habit

1

of keeping a pen or pencil near this book at all times, since you'll be doing some writing every day.

Now, in a few brief sentences, write down what you think motivation is.

_____

_____

_____

What kind of words did you use? Many people describe motivation as "the *desire* to do something," "the *willingness* to work toward a goal," or "the *force* that makes you do things."

Few of them describe motivation as a *process* that can be learned, or an *ability*, present in each and every one of us, that can be developed.

In other words, many people who want to diet unnecessarily doom themselves for one simple reason: They don't understand what motivation is. They don't know how to gain access to their own motivation and they don't know how to develop it.

Think of these people as contestants in a long-distance road race. Each has been given a car but has never been taught how to drive. All around them, they see other contestants whizzing by in cars while they themselves must walk. "Those lucky people," the walkers think. "They were born with the gift of driving!"

If you are one of the walkers, you are now going to learn how to drive. I am going to take the mystical robes off motivation and show you how to get it, keep it, and make it work for you.

Giving Up Your Misconceptions

First of all, let's get rid of your misconceptions about motivation.

This may not be as easy as you think. It's quite possible that you have a vested interest in hanging on to your old beliefs.

A patient of mine named Karin was extremely attached to the belief that motivation, like brown eyes or small feet, is something you're born with. "I come from a family of high achievers," she told me, "but the gene missed me. You know the old cliché about the smart one and the pretty one? Well, my sister was *both* the smart one and the pretty one. I never did well at school, I've never accomplished anything great, and I've never been able to lose weight. Motivation just isn't part of my makeup."

At first, it seemed that Karin was being remorselessly hard on herself. She wasn't nearly the unaccomplished slug she made herself out to be. I pointed out that, though she may not have gotten a Ph.D. (as her sister had), she had raised three children, she ran a home and had a successful marriage that, after twenty-three years, was still going strong. These are accomplishments in any-one's book, life achievements that obviously took the motivation Karin be-lieved she'd been born without.

When you look at Karin's reasoning closely, you will see why she clung so persistently to the idea that motivation is God-given. As long as she operated out of that belief, she was free of responsibility. *"I don't have the gift of moti-vation, so of course I can't control my eating,"* was her philosophy.

She didn't want to accept the idea that motivation is a process that can be learned because that would make her—once and for all—responsible for her eating. It would put the choice to work towards slimness or to remain heavy in her hands and hers alone.

It took a while for Karin to face the truth. Part of her difficulty was that she doubted her ability to succeed. She was convinced that even if she made the decision to take responsibility, she would turn out to be the one person in the world for whom my techniques would not work. In the end, she trusted both herself and me enough to make the jump. She finally became ready to give up her old concept of motivation. She was willing to learn a new definition of the word.

"If you're ready to do those two things," I told her, "then you're ready to lose weight." And she did: thirty-seven pounds.

Are you ready to give up your old understanding of motivation? Are you ready to learn a new way of thinking about it?

(Your answer) _____

If you answered "yes," then keep reading—you, too, are ready to lose weight.

The Mechanics of Motivation

Motivation isn't just a psychological phenomenon. Medical research indicates that it's very much physiologically based as well. Motivation originates in two specific areas of the brain, and certain definite changes occur in your body when you experience it. It's a process that can be identified and—most important of all—one that can be improved with practice.

You may already be familiar with the concept that certain brain functions can be developed and improved. Think, for example, of the person who has had a stroke and lost the power of speech. At first it would seem that this person is doomed to a future of silence, but it isn't always the case. Previously underutilized areas of the brain can be called into use. Initially the person struggles through each therapy session, groping for words and trying to shape the sounds he or she once knew so well. With practice speech becomes easier and easier, because the parts of the brain involved have been getting better accustomed to this particular task.

A similar chain of events occurs with motivation. You may struggle at first to "throw the switch" that activates your resolve. You may think "I'm just not getting it." But if you do not give up the moment will come: You will realize that you have tapped into your motivation.

Once you are able to recognize this, you will be able to get in touch with your motivation more and more easily. You will see that particular techniques work as triggers and you will be able to activate your motivation by using these triggers.

As you become more practiced, the process will seem almost automatic to you, just as driving a car seems natural to the one who knows how, while still baffling to the one who doesn't.

The best part of all is that each time you succeed in activating your motivation, you also strengthen and develop it. You will no longer be searching for a weak little beam of willpower—you will be throwing the switch on a powerful searchlight!

Recognizing Your Motivation

Remember Ike, whom I quoted at the beginning of this chapter? He claimed to have "no motivation at all" when it came to controlling his eating. Yet there he was in my office. Something inside Ike had compelled him to make an appointment and find his way to me. That something, even though Ike didn't acknowledge it, *was* motivation.

It's true that some people aren't motivated to lose weight. Until they become motivated, there's nothing at all that can be done for them. You can't wave a magic wand to make them care about their bodies and their health. But if someone has even a little ember of motivation, I can show them how to fan that spark into a bright and sturdy flame.

Let's look at you.

You picked up this book, opened the cover, and have now been reading for approximately a quarter of an hour. You could have picked up a romance book or a magazine instead. You could have decided to spend this time eating yet another piece of the food you know is bad for your health.

But you didn't.

You made a number of choices and took a series of actions that brought you, today, this very moment, to this particular place. What's behind that chain of choices and actions?

Motivation. *Your* motivation.

It's very important that you acknowledge this fact. Perhaps your motivation to control your eating has been dormant for a very long time. Perhaps you've never seen it before.

Take a few moments to get acquainted with it. I want you to see your motivation as a very real and very important part of yourself. Make your motivation feel welcome and get comfortable with it—you'll be seeing a lot of it in the days and weeks to come.

Here's an exercise that many of my patients find helpful and enjoyable. It encourages them to visualize their motivation in a specific way. Try giving your motivation a "personality" of its own—see it as something highly desirable that you would not like to be without.

If you are an animal lover, for example, you may feel that your motivation is a protective and affectionate pet: a dog or cat that will now be with you at all times. One of my male clients saw his motivation as the car of his dreams, a racy Lamborgini that, he said, "was powerful enough to carry him away from food cravings." A pianist I once treated described her motivation as beautiful music that made her feel strong and at peace with herself.

Use the space below to describe your motivation. Let your imagination play with the idea and have a good time.

My Motivation

_____

_____

_____

_____

_____

_____

_____

Tuning In to Your Personal Motivational Channel (PMC)

Are you ready to do just a bit more work on motivation today?

(Your answer) _____

Good. I'm glad you're willing to invest your time and energy—it's a sure sign that you're ready for success!

This next exercise isn't hard at all. Just read each of the three paragraphs below. Don't worry about agreeing or disagreeing or trying to "learn" the lesson of each one. Keep your mind open, allowing each paragraph to speak to you in its own particular way.

Paragraph I

Picture yourself losing weight and keeping it off for the rest of your life. Dubious? Well, seeing is believing! The 10-day diet countdown will show you how to make your excess weight disappear forever. It will show you how to look better than you have ever looked before. With this book to point the way, you'll see the issue of overeating in a new light. For the first time, you'll be able to draw the line at fattening snacks and second helpings. Imagine being slim and in the pink of health! All you have to do is get a new point of view on a very old problem—then watch your extra pounds melt away!

Paragraph II

I know you're busy, but can we talk for a few minutes? Please don't turn a deaf ear to me. I have something to say that will sound too good to be true—yet it is. You can lose weight by tuning in to the inner rhythms of your body. It's true! You can learn to listen to your body's hunger, not appetite, to keep from overeating. This book will tell you what techniques to use to keep your mind in harmony with your body. These techniques work because they echo your own desire to lose weight. Soon, an inner alarm will ring whenever you're tempted to binge. All you have to do is listen to your guiding voice and you'll be singing with health before you know it!

Paragraph III

If you're like many dieters, you've probably been trying to get a grip on your eating for some time. I understand exactly how you feel. Being out of touch with your body is painful. Well, it's time to forget about the agony of defeat and start enjoying the thrill of victory! You don't have to be alone or afraid because this book will "hold your hand" every step of the way. Many of its techniques will soothe you and eliminate tension. Soon you will be liberated from the compulsion to overeat. You won't feel hungry or empty, either. Instead, you'll be full of self-confidence and pleasure! Now, aren't you eager to take off?

Each of these paragraphs presents essentially the same information. I address you in a very direct way, telling you that this book has something valuable to teach you, something that will allow you to gain control of your eating and achieve the slim, healthy body you want. Yet chances are that one of these paragraphs seems more compelling to you than the others.

Use your pencil to rate the three passages, giving a 1 to the one that seems strongest and a 3 to the one that seems least persuasive:

____ Paragraph I
____ Paragraph II
____ Paragraph III

Why do these three similar paragraphs produce different reactions in you? Because each passage has been written to appeal to a different channel of communication.

Look again at Paragraph I. Is this the passage that *appears* strongest to you?

If you *glance* again at the passage, you will *see* that I use a lot of *sight* words in it, just as I am doing here. Let's *examine* the evidence:

Paragraph I

Picture yourself losing weight and keeping it off for the rest of your life. Dubious? Well, *seeing* is believing! The 10-day diet countdown will *show* you how to make your excess weight *disappear* forever. It will *show* you how to *look* better than you have ever *looked* before. With this book to *point the way*, you'll *see* the issue of overeating in a new *light*. For the first time, you'll be able to *draw the line* at fattening snacks and second helpings. *Imagine* being slim and in the *pink* of health! All you have to do is get a new *point of view* on a very old problem—then *watch* your extra pounds melt away!

If this paragraph is most effective for you, then your Personal Motivational Channel (PMC) is a *visual* one.

Or was it Paragraph II that *spoke* to you most strongly? Here's what I *said* in that passage:

Paragraph II

I know you're busy, but can we *talk* for a few minutes? Please don't *turn a deaf ear* to me. I have something to *say* that will *sound* too good to be true—yet it is. You can lose weight by *tuning in* to the inner *rhythms* of your body. It's true! You can learn to *listen* to your body's hunger, not appetite, to keep from overeating. This book will *tell* you what techniques to use to keep your mind in *harmony* with your body. These techniques work because they *echo* your own desire to lose weight. Soon, an inner *alarm will ring* whenever you're tempted to binge. All you have to do is *listen* to your guiding *voice* and you'll be *singing* with health before you know it!

Do you hear the message loud and clear? If this passage cries out for your attention, then your PMC is an *auditory* one.

Perhaps it was the third choice, Paragraph III, that *grabbed* you. In this passage, I used a lot of *feeling* words. Some of them you may have been aware of, but others might have *slipped* by you. Here's the passage one more time:

Paragraph III

If you're like many dieters, you've probably been trying to *get a grip* on your eating for some time. I *understand* exactly how you *feel*. Being *out of touch* with your body is *painful*. Well, it's time to forget about the *agony* of defeat and start *enjoying* the *thrill* of victory! You don't have to be *alone* or *afraid* because this book will *"hold your hand"* every step of the way. Many of its techniques will *soothe* you and eliminate *tension*. Soon you will be *liberated* from the *compulsion* to overeat. You won't *feel hungry* or *empty*, either. Instead, you'll be *full of self-confidence* and *pleasure!* Now, aren't you *eager* to take off?

If this is the passage that presses your buttons, than your PMC is a *feeling-oriented* one.

Why This Program Will Work for You

The exercise we've just done has taught you a lot. First, you have learned that not all people are equally receptive to the same words, images, and thoughts. Second, you have learned what particular kinds of words, images, and thoughts *you* are most receptive to. You have learned whether your Personal Motivational Channel—the channel through which you will tap into your motivation—is visual, auditory, or feeling-oriented.

Let's identify that channel right now.

I, _____, can tap into my motivation most effectively by using words, images, and thoughts that are _____ in nature.

In the course of the next ten days you will learn many techniques and many tools. But, valuable as they are, these tools and techniques are only raw materials. You will be given the pattern to follow but in each case you will make the finished product your own by completing it in your own way.

Now that you know your PMC, you can fashion tools and techniques that will be uniquely effective for you. Included in this book are numerous exercises and blank pages for you to fill in. Whenever you are asked to complete an exercise, do so with your Personal Motivational Channel in mind. Try to write in the "language" that is most effective for you and look for ways to tap into your own special channel.

If I ask you to visualize something, for example, you may decide to do just that—you may see yourself as you will look after your diet. Or you may "visualize" in an auditory way by making a cassette tape for yourself, a tape on which you hear your own voice encouraging you to succeed. Or your "visualization" may focus on feelings—what it will be like to feel slim and healthy, how wonderful it will be to enjoy your new body.

The techniques you are about to learn are proven. I have used them hundreds of times to help hundreds of patients lose weight and keep it off. By learning these techniques and making them your own, you too will succeed. Step by step, slowly at first but with increasing ease, you will discover how to activate and develop your motivation—the force that will allow you, at long last, to achieve your goal of healthful, permanent weight loss!

DAY ONE

SELF-AWARENESS DAY

Today's the day to:

- Set your Take-Off Day.
- Begin your 7-Day Food Diary.
- Fill out your Personal Inventory Chart.
- Analyze your Personal Inventory Chart.

TODAY'S THE first day of your 10-day diet countdown. It's the day you set your Take-Off Day and take the first step toward a healthier, slimmer self. In many ways it's the most important, most exciting day of the countdown because it's the day you put your commitment into action and the day you are given the tools that will make that commitment work.

If you are not ready to begin your diet ten days from today, *stop*. Do not go on. This book has been carefully designed to build your motivation over a controlled period of time. It's essential that you do not begin this program until you have firmly committed to a Take-Off Day.

Have you made that commitment? Good. Let's see how it looks in writing.

My Take-Off Day is _____ . By the time I reach it, I will be fully prepared. I will be armed with the motivational techniques this book is going to teach
me during the 10-day diet countdown. Already, I am beginning to look forward to
this date because it marks a positive change in my life.

_____
(Signature)

The First Step

Many patients come into my office feeling overwhelmed and helpless about
their weight. "I have to lose fifty pounds," one woman despaired. "I'd rather
move a mountain."

"If I asked you to move a mountain, how would you do it?" I asked her.

After thinking for just a moment she grinned and answered, "One shov-
elful at a time, I guess."

It was important for her to realize then that losing weight was really no
different from moving that imaginary mountain. It was a task that had to be
approached and accomplished *one step at a time.*

And one step at a time, learning and gaining confidence as you go, is how
you will succeed. If you have failed at past attempts to diet, it's probably because you tried to go directly from step A to finished product Z. You wanted
to be perfect overnight: to change your eating habits, your attitudes, and your
body image all at once. This is like trying to haul a mountain by lassoing it
and pulling on the rope. Naturally, your motivation was crushed in the attempt.

This 10-day diet countdown won't crush your motivation. It will
strengthen it by leading you from step A to step B, from step B to step C, and

so on. You won't be told to do something without first being taught how to do it.

If you are like most of my patients, you are already beginning to feel more relaxed. That's important because you and I are going to spend some time working together. I'm interested in you. I want to get to know you and your daily routines. How do you begin each day? Do you take time to groom and care for yourself or do you plunge right ahead without really taking time for yourself?

Of course, since you've come to me for help, there's a reason why I'm asking you these questions. I want to understand how you feel about yourself and what your eating patterns are. This kind of information is needed before we can decide together what must be changed.

The 7-Day Food Diary

Many people with weight problems are truly unaware of their eating habits. They take moderate portions at meals and may even leave food on their plates. Yet often they're consuming a high number of calories between meals, in the course of food preparation, or in alcoholic beverages.

To help my patients identify their eating patterns, I give each one a 7-Day Food Diary. Your own diary begins on page 18 and will continue each day for the next seven days.

The rules for filling it out are very simple. Keep track of every bit that goes into your mouth: the foods you eat at breakfast, lunch, and dinner, as well as the spoon you lick while making spaghetti sauce, the corn chips you munch from your child's plate, and the glass of wine you drink with your mate before dinner. As accurately as possible, note the time of day you ate the food and how much you ate. If there were significant feelings attached to the eating experience, make a note of them as well.

"A food diary! What a unique and wonderful idea! Thank you! I can hardly wait to begin!"

That's the kind of response I've yet to hear. Many veterans of the diet wars have been asked to keep such diaries in the past. You too? If so, you probably either didn't bother with it or, after a few days, let the diary lapse.

I can't really blame you. Keeping a food diary is a tough assignment. It's boring. It takes time. It robs you of the myth that you really don't eat all that much. Unless you understand why it's important to keep a food diary, your resolve will once again be crushed. So let's take a minute to build your motivation. Let's see what's in this for you.

Your goal right now is to get yourself motivated to lose weight permanently. Think of that weight as a mountain that needs to be moved. Would you rather move that mountain with tools or with nothing but your bare hands?

One of your most valuable tools is awareness. If you keep your 7-Day Food Diary faithfully, accurately, and honestly, you will gain that tool. You will become aware of your own eating patterns. Perhaps you are someone who eats quite sensibly during the day only to lose control at night. Or you may be one of the many who skip breakfast only to grab a calorie-laden pastry at midmorning. Or your 7-Day Food Diary may reveal that you often eat to relieve unpleasant emotions such as anxiety, frustration, anger, boredom, or loneliness.

Katie, one of my earliest patients, credits her food diary with helping her come to terms with her destructive eating habits for the first time in her life. As a child, Katie's mother had constantly worried that Katie would gain too much weight. Every bite Katie took was scrutinized and worried over, and Katie, a normal child with a normal child's appetite, often left the table feeling hungry and resentful.

By the time Katie was an adult, she had reached the unconscious conclusion that her appetite was abnormally large. If she ate enough to satisfy herself, she felt, people would be shocked. In her own home, she took precautions to save herself from this humiliation. As she prepared meals for her husband she would snack on whatever was at hand. Then, with her husband, she would sit down and eat a normal meal, her husband not knowing that this was actually her second meal.

By keeping a food diary, Katie realized what she was doing wrong, and only then could she adhere to a sensible eating schedule. Katie also realized that her appetite wasn't abnormally large. Quite often, she was full by the time she sat down to eat. "But of course, since the food was there, I ate anyway." It wasn't true hunger that was driving Katie to overeat but a *fear* of hunger rooted in the distant past. Once she saw the pattern clearly, she was able to break the destructive cycle.

How? Some of the strategies I helped Katie devise were very simple, such as developing a willingness to experience hunger, or deciding to eliminate certain foods from her diet. Other strategies had nothing to do with food. They were based on refocusing and behavior-modification techniques, the same techniques you will learn later in this book.

As you keep your own 7-Day Food Diary you will see what your own trouble spots are and, like Katie, learn to overcome them.

Remember, you are not being asked to keep this diary forever, or even to keep it for the entire 10-day countdown. Keep it for only seven days, one day at a time. (But if it helps you to take control of your food intake, then of course you may continue it as long as you wish.)

Now that you see how keeping a 7-Day Food Diary will help you toward your goal, are you willing to do it?

(Your answer) _____

If you answered "yes," congratulations! Your motivation just got stronger. Before going on to Day 1 of your 7-Day Food Diary, take a moment to enjoy your new feeling of power and control.

7-DAY FOOD DIARY

For each entry, include the food you ate as well as any beverage, the time and circumstances, and any important feelings you had.

DAY 1

Day _____ Date _____

Breakfast _____

_____

Between _____

_____

Lunch _____

_____

Between _____

_____

Dinner _____

_____

Between _____

_____

Thoughts _____

_____

_____

Your Personal Inventory Chart

When it comes to identifying a problem and making a change, insight is one of the most important tools anyone can have. That tool must be as powerful as possible. You have to be able to trust it and rely on it.

Not all the insight you need will come through your 7-Day Food Diary. That's why I've provided a Personal Inventory Chart as well. You will find your copy on pages 20–23. Can you set aside twenty or thirty minutes today to fill it out?

(Your answer) _____

You will find this a much less demanding assignment than keeping a food diary! Just fill out your Personal Inventory Chart honestly, without worrying about right or wrong responses. Don't leave any question unanswered: Write either yes, no, or don't know in each blank. Don't try to figure out what your answers mean as you go along. After you've completed the inventory, we'll look at the results together.

PERSONAL INVENTORY CHART

Date _____ Height _____ Weight _____

I. WEIGHT HISTORY

As a child were you normal weight? Overweight? Underweight?

_____

How about as a teenager? _____

Would you classify yourself as someone who has always been heavy or as some-one whose weight has been normal most of the time?

_____

Have you had any episodes of extreme weight fluctuations?

_____

If you answered yes to the above question, describe them briefly.

_____

_____

When was the last time you were at a normal weight? How long did you maintain your ideal body weight?

_____

_____

Can you remember a time during which you gained a significant amount of weight? If so, when was it? What else was going on in your life at the time?

_____

Do you consider yourself a positive person or a negative person? _____

Are you happy most of the time or do you have frequent bouts of sadness and despair?

_____

_____

Do you consider yourself an active or a passive person?

_____

Do you have a light, moderate, or high physical activity level? _____

II. FOOD HISTORY

If you had to identify the source of your problem, would you say that you: (If more than one choice applies, use numbers to indicate the main source of the problem and the less important sources.)

_____ Eat the same foods and quantities that most other people eat but gain weight when other people do not.

_____ Eat a greater quantity of all foods than is normal.

_____ Eat an average quantity of most foods but overindulge in a few foods (such as sweets, breads, etc.).

_____ Eat the same foods and amounts you have always eaten but have experienced a recent weight gain.

_____ Eat when you are not truly hungry.

Can you remember a time when you used food as a reward, as a way of cheering yourself up, as a way of getting rid of stress, boredom, etc. ? Describe.

_____

_____

_____

_____

How often do you use food in this way? _____

_____

Have you ever binged on food? What did you eat? Can you remember what triggered the binge? Can you recall your feelings? How often has this happened to you?

_____

_____

_____

III. DIET HISTORY

If you're like most people who want to lose weight, you've dieted before. List each significant diet experience.

First Diet _____

Type of Diet _____

How long was the diet followed? _____

What were the results? _____

Were you satisfied? _____

If you went off the diet before you planned to, why? _____

_____

How long were you able to maintain your weight loss? _____

_____

Would this be a good diet for you to use again? Why or why not? _____

_____

Second Diet _____

Type of Diet _____

How long was the diet followed? _____

What were the results? _____

Were you satisfied? _____

If you went off the diet before you planned to, why? _____

_____

How long were you able to maintain your weight loss? _____

_____

Would this be a good diet for you to use again? Why or why not? _____

_____

What Your Personal Inventory Chart Tells You

Before you can take control of a situation, you need to know what the situation is and what brought it about.

Your situation, of course, is that you have decided to lose a certain amount of weight. But where did that weight come from? Why and how have you put it on?

One of the biggest myths of the twentieth century is that people overeat because they are deeply unhappy, frustrated, neurotic, or otherwise psychologically impaired. It's true that some people do overeat for reasons that are purely psychological. But not every overweight person falls into this category.

In the course of my work I have discovered that overweight is one problem with many sources. Here are the six main reasons why people gain excess weight:

- *Genetic predisposition.* Not all bodies handle calories in the same way. Some people are genetically predisposed to gain more weight on fewer calories than other people. If you come from a family with several obese members, you probably fall into this category. Does this mean you are destined to be overweight? Not at all. By working with your doctor, you can find a diet that allows you to lose weight. If you do fall into this category, realize that your challenge will always be greater: You must spend your calories wisely, making sure the foods you eat meet your body's basic nutritional needs. A regular schedule of exercise is a *must* if you want to maintain a lower body weight.
- *Poor eating habits.* There are two reasons why people have poor eating habits. One is that some of us have simply become lazy about the way we eat. We know a good deal about nutrition but don't put that knowledge to use. We eat what's readily available or what appeals to us at the moment. The second reason is that some people are truly in the dark about the nutritional content of foods. They do not realize, for example, that certain snacks and convenience foods are loaded with fats, salt, and sugar. People with poor eating habits must learn to identify and change their eating patterns, which have taken a lifetime to form. That is what this book is all about!
- *Change of lifestyle.* Why do people who have maintained a normal weight for years suddenly gain? One reason can be a change in lifestyle. The formerly active wife and mother who resumes her office career may find that those sedentary hours add extra pounds. Even a less drastic change, like moving from a two-story house to a house with no stairs to climb, can make a difference. Examine your lifestyle for changes in activity levels and adjust your habits

accordingly. Look for new situations and conditions that may be prompting you to eat more than you once did.

- *Change of physical condition.* Even healthy people undergo physical changes that cause weight gains. For many women, pregnancy results in extra pounds. For men and women both, the simple act of maturing demands a change in eating habits. During adolescence, your need for calories is at an all-time high. As you move through adulthood and into middle age, you need fewer and fewer calories. If you don't decrease your food intake accordingly, you will wind up with unwanted pounds. For some women, menopause can be an especially dangerous time. (Others, it should be noted, report renewed energy and vitality during this time.)

Using aging or menopause as an excuse to gain weight, however, is just that—an excuse. By learning what your body's true requirements are, you will be able to maintain a healthy weight.

- *Taking medication.* This is another factor that is sometimes overlooked. A number of regularly prescribed drugs have side effects that may contribute to weight gain. If you are on medication of any sort, discuss it with your doctor. Make sure he or she knows of your plans to lose weight and approves the diet you have chosen. Remember that a person of normal weight who is laid up with a medical condition will gain weight because of decreased activity.

- *Using food for psychological reasons.* Whenever you eat other than to satisfy true hunger, you are eating for psychological reasons. Does this mean you have deep-rooted psychological problems? Probably not. We live in a society in which food is not merely a bare necessity but a form of entertainment as well. The number of new foods that come onto the market each year is truly astonishing, and it is my belief that almost everyone, at some time, eats for reasons that are psychological. When is this a problem? When it becomes a repetitive pattern, when it results in a weight gain, or when food begins to replace friends, love, work, or other activities. The person who has a psychological relationship with food needs a two-pronged approach to weight loss, one that combines diet with behavior and attitudinal changes. That two-pronged approach is what this book is all about.

• *Using overweight for psychological reasons.* I have yet to meet the person who consciously wants to be overweight. But the truth is that many people who have excess weight have a vested interest in holding on to it. For some, it's a buffer against the world, an excuse for not facing a fear of rejection. For others, a sign of rebellious individualism. For still others, it's a filtering device to keep superficial, looks-obsessed people away. And still, for some, excess weight is a badge of success, wealth, and plentitude.

Occasionally, overweight is a sign of confusion over body image and mental identification, such as in the patient I once treated who identified with her father, who was heavy, strong, and powerful. Like the person who has a psychological relationship with food, the person who's having a secret affair with overweight will especially benefit from the two-pronged approach of this book.

Once you understand why you have gained, you will be able to choose a successful method of losing weight and keeping it off. Someone who eats for psychological reasons, for example, might find Overeaters Anonymous a far more effective program than any other because it addresses this particular problem. A person who is genetically predisposed to gain weight might profit most from a weight reduction program under the supervision of a physician. And a person who has bad eating habits will probably want to pay particular attention to reprogramming his or her behavior through techniques such as those outlined later in this book.

The Personal Inventory Chart is designed to show you how much you do—or don't—know about your weight problem. You may find that you know a great deal. Or, as we continue our ten-day journey together, you may find you have quite a few mistaken notions about your body and your eating habits.

Each section of the chart supplies you with important information. Look at your answers to the first part of the chart, "Weight History." If you have always been overweight, even as a child, you may be someone who is genetically predisposed to gain weight. If, on the other hand, you have gained weight during periods of stress, you have probably used food for psychological reasons.

Other answers may reveal a change of lifestyle you were previously unaware of, or simply a lapse of good eating habits.

The next part of the chart, "Food History," will further clarify the problem. Do you eat an average diet but gain weight anyway? You may be leading a far too sedentary lifestyle, one that provides no opportunity for you to burn calories. Or you may be genetically predisposed to overweight or the "victim" of a sudden shift in lifestyle or physical condition. (You may also, of course, have developed bad eating habits that you are unaware of or have denied until now. If that's the case, your 7-Day Food Diary will put you in touch with the truth.) If you eat when you are not hungry and have misused food (as a reward, stress-breaker, etc.), you will be especially interested in Day 9, when together we'll design a new reward system and choose alternative ways of coping with discomfort. And, if bingeing is part of your problem, you'll want to identify the foods that trigger a binge and eliminate them from your diet.

Now go on to the "Diet History" section. The best diet (provided it's nutritionally sound, of course) is almost always the one that has worked for you before. A diet that you were able to follow, even if the results were slow in coming, is better than a diet that was so drastic you gave up after two or three days. *No matter what a diet's claims are, no matter how well it's worked for others, it's only effective if it works for you.*

It's important to look at both your dieting successes and your dieting failures. One of the things that troubles me most is seeing people label themselves "hopeless" and "weak-willed" when the real problem is that they've chosen a diet that's all wrong for them. The harried working mother who can't find time to prepare special low-calorie meals may do quite well with preprepared products. The person who binges on certain foods may need a diet that eliminates these foods—and the temptation to binge on them—completely. Still another person may need programs such as Overeaters Anonymous or Weight Watchers, which offer supportive group environments.

In evaluating your successes and failures, remember that how long you maintained your weight loss is important. A diet that takes off weight too quickly and does not provide a program for maintenance may have a rebound effect that leads you to regain weight just as quickly as you lost it.

During the 10-day diet countdown you'll learn to focus yourself *away* from food and *toward* other parts of your life. These techniques will work most effectively if you have chosen a diet suited to your individual problem. On pages 211–217 you will find a copy of a diet that will meet your body's nutritional needs and satisfy true physical hunger. A brief evaluation of other diet programs can be found in Appendix I. You don't have to decide today which diet you want to go on. But do use the next few days to shop for one that suits you, just as you would shop for a glamorous dress or a new sports car.

One More Step

The last step I would like you to take today is very simple. It requires no more than a phone call to your family doctor. *Before you begin any diet program, it's important to have a physical checkup.*

Most people can quote this statement word for word. They've heard it a thousand times from concerned friends, magazine articles, exercise gurus, their own doctors, and weight-loss experts.

But they've never followed the advice.

You may not, either. I can't take your hand and lead you to your doctor. But I can tell you that if you were to visit me in my office, I wouldn't treat you without giving you a physical exam.

I hope by now you trust me enough to know I wouldn't ask you to do something just for form's sake. Will you read why I think a physical exam is so important?

(Your answer) ——————————————————————

Occasionally, excess weight points to an underlying medical problem (such as diabetes or an underactive thyroid) requiring medical attention. Even if your extra pounds are due to simple overeating, carrying too much weight can give rise to high blood pressure, heart disease, and other conditions that require treatment.

Your doctor may already have been nagging you to lose weight for these very reasons, and so you have come to view him or her as the enemy. Now that you've decided to lose weight, however, the enemy will become your ally. Your doctor will be able to assess your overall fitness, help you set your goal weight, and recommend a diet that will be safe as well as effective. And, once you know you're in good health, you won't be able to blame your "glands" for keeping you heavy.

There's another reason why a checkup is important. You need to find out what level of physical activity you're capable of. It's true that exercise alone will not make you lose weight—you must change your eating patterns too. However, exercise is a tremendous tool, one you should be able to make full use of, and that's something you can't do if you're worried about your true fitness level.

Hey! You Did It!

You made it through Day 1! Maybe you didn't think you would. Or maybe you think you did only because Day 1 is the "easy" day, the day you get ready for all the hard days to follow.

Let me tell you right now that Day 1 is the hardest, not the easiest, because it's the day you have to commit to a Take-Off Day. Not only did you do that today, but you began your 7-Day Food Diary and filled out your Personal Inventory Chart as well. If you completed this day, you will be able to complete each of the remaining days of the 10-day diet countdown. In fact, the remaining days will become easier as your motivation builds and you master this book's techniques.

So just take one more minute to read, enjoy, and sign the affidavit on the following page.

I, _____, congratulate myself. I didn't just buy *Your Diet Coach* and put it on a shelf. I made a commitment and stuck with it. I completed Day 1. In just this way, one step at a time, I will be able to keep on going until I reach my goal.

_____

(Signature)

DAY TWO

EATING AWARENESS DAY

Today's the day to:

- Reaffirm your Take-Off Day.
- Complete Day 2 of your 7-Day Food Diary.
- "Observe" yourself eating a typical meal.
- Begin to target your destructive eating patterns.

Nine Days and Counting

BEFORE WE BEGIN today's activities, let's look into the future for a moment. Take-Off Day is nine days away. How do you feel about that?

(Your answer) _____

Many people set a day to diet and look forward to it with about as much enthusiasm as they look forward to root-canal work. They picture a day that marks the beginning of deprivation and an end to "good times."

Is it any wonder that by the end of the first day they are hungry, angry, and emotionally exhausted?

If you regard dieting as a walk on the edge of starvation as you skirt the forests of resentment and dip into the lagoon of despair, that's what it will be for you.

Not only does dieting not have to be this way, it *shouldn't* be this way.

True, doing without the foods you are accustomed to is uncomfortable. That's why I suggest my patients look at their new diet as an exciting learning

31

experience in which they will discover new foods, new tastes, textures, and sensations.

Are you comfortable right now? Do you find satisfaction in the way your body looks and feels? Do you feel good after each meal? Do you feel in control of your eating?

If the answer to these questions was yes, you would never have picked up this book. You would never have come this far with me. So instead of focusing on what you'll be doing without on Take-Off Day, I want you to begin focusing on the feelings you'll be enjoying.

- On Take-Off Day, I will savor the knowledge that I'm doing what's right for my body and my life.

- On Take-Off Day, I will begin to take pleasure in my body once again.

- On Take-Off Day, I will feel satisfied—not miserable and stuffed—after each meal.

- On Take-Off Day, I will know the relief of being in control of my eating.

Come back to these thoughts often today. By the time you go to bed tonight, you will have begun to realize that Take-Off Day is not a day of deprivation. It is the day you liberate yourself from guilt, discomfort, and despair. It's the day you begin to enjoy feeling good once again.

Complete Day 2 of Your 7-Day Food Diary

Today, just as you did yesterday, continue to fill in your 7-Day Food Diary. Remember to be completely honest in writing down *all* the food you eat, as well as the quantity, the time of day, the circumstances, and any important feelings surrounding the experience.

7-DAY FOOD DIARY

For each entry, include the food you ate as well as all beverages, the time and circumstances, and any important feelings you had.

DAY 2

Day _____ Date _____

Breakfast _____

_____

Between _____

_____

Lunch _____

_____

Between _____

_____

Dinner _____

_____

Between _____

_____

Thoughts _____

_____

_____

Make a Date to Dine

Today, make a dining date with yourself. It can be for breakfast, lunch, or dinner. I want you to step outside of yourself mentally and watch yourself eat. This exercise, like the task of keeping a 7-Day Food Diary, will help you become aware of the eating habits you want to break free of.

To get the most from this exercise, pick a meal that is representative of your normal eating patterns. If you often eat alone, don't pick the one meal of the week when you eat with friends. If you most often prepare your own meals, don't pick a meal when you dine out. And if you skip breakfast every single weekday, try not to pick a weekend breakfast.

Is there a particular meal of the day that is almost always difficult for you? By difficult, I mean the meal at which you most often lose control of your eating. If so, try to target that meal.

Perhaps the idea of this exercise is confusing or even intimidating to you. How can you do something and watch yourself do it at the same time? Do you need to have developed skills of yoga, astral projection, or some other abstract philosophy to accomplish it?

Not at all. As I told you at the very beginning of this book, you will not be asked to do anything you aren't capable of doing. In fact, this exercise won't be much different from the 7-Day Food Diary you are already becoming accustomed to.

Are you ready?

(Your answer) _____

Observe Yourself As You Eat a Typical Meal

On pages 37–45 you'll find your Eating Awareness Inventory. I've prepared it in order to help you become aware of the eating habits you have developed over the years. The information it will provide, together with the data you are gathering in your 7-Day Food Diary, will reveal your destructive eating patterns to you.

Don't look at the questions in this inventory in advance. Doing so may make you so self-conscious it will subconsciously alter your ordinary behavior. If possible, complete each section of the chart as you complete that phase of the meal. If that isn't possible, complete the entire inventory immediately after the meal.

Throughout this meal, watch yourself with an honest and objective eye.

Perhaps this seems impossible to you. How can you be both the participant and the observer of your own actions? It isn't as difficult as you think. Here's a five-point plan to ensure your success:

- *State your intentions.* As you begin this experiment, say to yourself, "I am going to observe myself preparing and eating this meal."
- *Stay in the here and now.* Do not become distracted by thinking over a conversation you had last night or anticipating an upcoming event. If you are eating with others, keep part of your awareness focused on yourself.
- *Think of your eye as a movie camera.* Imagine that the scene before you is a film unfolding scene by scene. Take in and evaluate the details as if you were seeing them for the very first time, just as you would in a real viewing situation.
- *Translate what you see into words.* If you see your hand reaching for a second handful of potato chips while the health salad lies still untouched on your plate, take time to think to yourself, "I am eating more of the food I like most before I have eaten any of the food I like least."
- *Avoid the pitfall of denial.* Don't disavow the truth of what you see by making excuses such as, "I ate it but I didn't mean to," "I only ate it because . . ." or "I wouldn't have eaten it if . . ." The point is you ate it. Period.

I'm sure you can perform this simple technique of self-observation but if you aren't sure, practice. Pick an action such as dressing yourself or performing some task and see how easy it is. Then apply the same methods to eating a typical meal.

You are now ready to move closer to your goal by completing the Eating Awareness Inventory on the following pages.

EATING AWARENESS INVENTORY

I. THE SELF-PREPARED MEAL

If you didn't prepare the meal yourself, go on to section II.

1. Did you prepare a nutritionally balanced meal? _____

2. Did you prepare what you had planned to prepare or did you deviate from your plan in some way?

_____ Prepared a planned meal?

_____ Deviated from a plan?

3. If you deviated from your plan, was the meal you ended up with as nutritious as the one originally planned?

_____

4. If you deviated from your plan, did you:

_____ Prepare more food items than planned?

_____ Prepare fewer food items than planned?

_____ Substitute food items?

5. List the foods you planned to prepare and didn't:

_____

_____

6. List the foods you prepared that you hadn't planned to:

_____

_____

7. Why did you prepare the foods you did? (Check all that apply)

_____ Good nutrition

_____ Economy

_____ Efficiency and/or convenience

_____ Enjoy the experience of cooking these foods

_____ Please others in the family

Craved particular foods. List: _____

_____

_____

_____

Other reasons. List: _____

_____

8. Did you snack, sample, or lick spoons as you prepared the meal? _____
9. If you ate while you prepared the meal, did you feel:

_____ Guilty?

_____ Angry or resentful?

_____ Happy?

_____ Disappointed over ruining your enjoyment of the meal?

_____ Other: _____

10. Did you prepare more food than was needed at this meal?

_____

11. If yes, how much extra food did you prepare?

_____ A little extra food?

_____ Some extra food?

_____ A lot of extra food?

12. What were your reasons for preparing extra food?

_____

_____

_____

13. If you prepared extra food, did you place the extra amount in serving dishes, leave it in the kitchen, or store it immediately?

_____

_____

_____

II. WHEN AND WHY?

1. Imagine that your stomach is a cup. When you began to eat this meal, was that cup:

_____ Empty?

_____ Half empty?

_____ Almost full?

2. Check your reasons for eating this meal:

_____ I was truly hungry.

_____ I craved one of the foods included in this meal.

_____ It was time to eat.

_____ I was afraid that I would be hungry later if I didn't eat.

_____ I needed a relaxation break.

_____ There was nothing else to do.

_____ To avoid doing something I didn't particularly want to do.

_____ To avoid thinking about something I didn't want to think about.

_____ Eating makes me happy.

_____ Others expected me to eat with them.

_____ It was my last chance to eat certain foods before going on my diet.

_____ Other: _____

_____

_____ Other: _____

_____

_____ Other: _____

_____

III. YOUR EATING STYLE

1. How much food did you put on your plate?

_____ Small portions?

_____ Average portions?

_____ Large portions?

2. Did you put all of the food you ate on your plate first or did you nibble directly from a serving plate?

_____

3. Did you serve yourself a variety of foods, including some foods you didn't like as well as others?

_____

4. List the foods at this meal that you didn't eat and your reasons for not eating them. _____

_____

_____

5. As you ate, did you alternate bites of different kinds of food or did you eat your favorite food first? _____

6. How much food did you put in your mouth at one time?

_____ A small amount?

_____ A manageable mouthful?

_____ Too much?

7. Did you chew thoroughly before swallowing? _____

8. If you were eating a sandwich, piece of fruit, or other hand-held item, did you put it down between bites?

_____

9. Did you put your knife, fork, and spoon down between bites? _____

10. Was your mouth completely empty before you picked up your fork to take another bite or were you pushing more food toward yourself before you were truly ready for it?

_____

11. Did you "wash down" mouthfuls of food with a beverage?

_____

12. Did you clean your plate, even if you were already somewhat full? _____

13. Did you take second helpings? _____

14. If you took second helpings, did you take second helpings of everything or only of certain foods? List:

_____

_____

15. If you took second helpings, did you:

_____ Refill your plate automatically?

_____ Wait a few minutes before deciding if you wanted more?

_____ Wait quite a while (fifteen minutes or more) before deciding you wanted more?

16. If you took second helpings, why? (Check all that apply)

_____ I was still truly hungry.

———— I was no longer truly hungry but was somewhat hungry.

———— I "had room" for more.

———— I almost always take second helpings.

———— I wanted to enjoy more of the taste of a certain food.

———— I wanted to prolong the pleasure of the meal.

———— Everyone else at the table was still eating.

———— I wanted to finish up what was in the serving dish.

IV. STOPPING

1. Once more, picture your stomach as a cup. Did you stop eating when the cup was:

———— Empty?

———— Half empty?

———— Almost full?

———— Spilling over?

2. How long did it take you to eat the meal? ————————————————

3. Did you eat more food at this meal than your body truly needed? ————
4. If yes, how much more?

———— A little more

———— Somewhat more

———— Much more

5. If you prepared or served more food than you expected to be eaten at this meal, was the amount of leftover food:

_____ More than you expected?

_____ About the same as you expected?

_____ Less than you expected?

6. When you were finished eating, did you feel emotionally let down, as if the highlight of the day was now over?

_____

7. After you finished eating, did you stop to think, "I am full and satisfied"?

_____

8. After you finished eating, did you find yourself looking forward to a snack you would have later or to the next meal you would eat?

_____

9. If yes, describe the foods you looked forward to, when you planned to eat them, and any activity you would be doing while you ate (such as watching television, etc.).

_____

_____

_____

10. Were you able to clear away the leftovers, wash the dishes, etc., without eating any more food?

_____

11. If no, describe the foods you ate and how you ate them:

_____

_____

_____

V. THE ACID TEST

Imagine this scenario: This meal, from preparation to cleanup, has been video-taped without your knowledge. At this moment copies of the tape are being rushed to everyone you know—from the person you love most to the mailman on your block.

1. How do you feel about people viewing this tape? Use the most colorful adjectives you can think of to describe your feelings.

_____

2. Describe what you did at this meal that you wouldn't want others to know about. Be honest. Be specific.

_____

_____

_____

_____

_____

_____

Eating Styles

Like almost anything in life, the process of change can be broken down into several logical steps. You have already taken the first step toward changing your eating patterns by setting your Take-Off Day and joining me in the 10-day diet countdown. The second step, of course, is to discover what needs to be changed. That is why I have asked you to keep a 7-Day Food Diary and to observe yourself eating a typical meal. The information you gather through these activities will help you see clearly, perhaps for the first time in your life, why you have gained weight.

Every one of us has an eating style. If you are overweight, you have developed an eating style that is destructive to your body, a style that works against your goal of losing weight. To reach your goal and to maintain it, you will have to replace your destructive eating style with one that is healthful.

I have observed a number of destructive eating styles common to overweight individuals. Here are the most common ones:

- *The fussy eater.* The fussy eater's problem is not in the quantity of food he eats, it's in its variety—or lack of it. Fussy eaters pick a few favorite foods, usually high calorie ones, and fill up on them. When others order salad and one slice of pizza, the fussy eater skips the salad and discovers he must eat two pieces of pizza to feel full.

- *The binge eater.* Like the alcoholic, the binge eater discovers that "one is too many and a thousand are not enough." Many binge eaters can exert control for periods of time or over certain types of food. The trouble begins when something triggers a binge (either a psychological factor such as stress, depression, etc., or proximity to a certain type of food). Then eating goes out of control. It should be noted that some physicians feel food allergies can trigger binges, setting up a craving for the very food one's body has trouble with.

- *The sneak eater.* The sneak eater might make an excellent stonecutter or sculptor: She can slice a hunk from a piece of cake so that you'll never know it's missing. Though overweight, this person seems conscientious about her eating. She can sit through an elaborate dinner party without reaching for seconds and can confidently decline dessert. The truth is, she doesn't need that puny piece of lemon pie because she's got a stash of chocolate mocha rum balls waiting for her at home. The sneak eater isn't just hiding her habits from her friends and family—she's hiding them from herself.

- ***The speed eater.*** If speed eating were an Olympic event, Americans would be bringing home a lot more gold. We live in a high-pressure world in which the clock always seems to be running. To get everything done on time, we've learned to race through life at top speed. The speed eater carries this pace to the dinner table with him and by the time he realizes he's full, he's already overeaten.

- ***The snacker.*** How can the snacker have gained weight? She hardly ever sits down to a full meal. And that's just the problem. Unless the snacker is munching on raw vegetables, fresh fruit, and other low-calorie items all day, she's probably taking in far more calories than she realizes. A piece of lunch meat, a handful of pretzels, a tumbler of papaya juice—it all adds up. But because the snacker never sees it on her plate, she loses track of how much she's eating and what she's eating.

- ***The impulse eater.*** The impulse eater is the advertising industry's dream. Show him a commercial for cookies and he's on his way to a kitchen. Let him walk by a pizza parlor and he's replanned his dinner. It isn't that the impulse eater plans to overeat; it's something that happens when he's not paying attention to what he's putting in his mouth.

- ***The weekend eater.*** Weekend eaters walk the straight and narrow during the week. They draw the line on fats, sugars, and other dietary nonsense. But when the weekend arrives, watch out. For them, relaxation is a four-letter word: F-O-O-D. Then Monday arrives and the weekend eater sets about trying to atone for the sins of the weekend. Unfortunately, forty-eight hours of non-stop indulgence can't be done away with so lightly.

- ***The response eater.*** Some people eat when they're hungry. Some people eat when happy. Some people eat when they're sad. Some people eat when they're nervous, frustrated, or under stress. The response eater eats for all of these reasons. For him, the first course of action to take in any situation is to feed himself, a habit that adds one more problem—overweight—to his life.

• *The social eater.* Good times, good friends, good food. As far as the social eater is concerned, they all go together. Unfortunately, foods eaten in social situations like parties and dinners out often tend to be loaded with calories. Foods the social eater wouldn't dream of eating by herself seem much more acceptable when her friends are eating them too. Unfortunately, the social eater doesn't know how to just say no. Quite often, she consumes more food than anyone else in the crowd. Another hazard of social eating: the high-calorie alcoholic beverages that often go with the fun.

• *The diet junkie.* For the diet junkie, eating is either feast or famine. He's either on a diet or planning to go on one. When he's dieting, he feels depressed and deprived. When he goes off a diet, he compensates by treating himself to all the foods he had to do without. Soon he's back to his old weight and facing another round of dieting. Often, he regains his weight and even more, as roller-coaster dieting can actually lead to progressively larger weight gains. The diet junkie's problem can be summed up in a few words: He can eat less food than required, he can eat more food than required, but he has never learned to feed his body what it needs to maintain a stable, healthy weight.

• *The rebellious eater.* The rebellious eater knows she should diet. Her loved ones urge her. Her doctor nags her. Her employer threatens her. Even her own conscience reminds her, as she reaches for a third hot biscuit, that she really *shouldn't* be eating so much. All to no avail. The lady in question is a rebel. Years of "helpful," "well-meaning" advice have left her simmering with rage. But she can't behead her husband for telling her to take off a few pounds, so the rebellious eater does the next best thing: To show the world it can't control her she continues to eat. And eat. And eat.

Perhaps, just two days into our journey together, you have already begun to see certain patterns emerge.

Right now, take a few minutes to write down your thoughts about your destructive eating style. Don't be rough or accusatory with yourself. It won't help at all to write "I am a hopeless binge eater" or "I pig out on cookies." These are negative messages and will actually reenforce your negative concept of yourself. Later, this book will show you how to replace negative messages with positive ones. Get into the habit right now by balancing each observation of a destructive habit with a statement of your commitment to change.

An example might be: "I often eat on impulse without really thinking of what I am doing, but by using the techniques in this book, I will learn to think first."

Or: "I have often eaten on the sly, hiding my eating style from others as well as from myself. I am no longer willing to turn a blind eye to my own destructive habits—I care too much to let this happen to me."

Or simply: "I have previously been a diet junkie, and this is the destructive eating style I am going to change."

Now that you've got the idea, take a few minutes to write down what you've learned about your eating style so far. Don't despair if your own habits still seem a mystery to you. You still have more data to gather and on Day 8, after you've completed your 7-Day Food Diary, we'll return for a look at your week-long patterns.

What I Know So Far

_____

_____

_____

_____

_____

_____

_____

_____

_____

_____

_____

Congratulations—Again!

If you were a gunslinger, you could put another notch on your belt. You've made it through two days of the 10-day diet countdown. By now, you're getting into the rhythm of what we're doing together. You're learning about yourself and you're learning to tackle your problem step by step by step. *Most of all, you're learning that this time you're really going to succeed!*

DAY
THREE

TOUCH-CONTROL DAY

Today's the day to:
- Reinforce your motivation.
- Complete Day 3 of your 7-Day Food Diary.
- Learn the Touch-Control Method.

YOU'VE DONE a lot of work in the past two days. Ready for a breather?

(Your answer) _____

I thought so. That's why I've lightened today's load. The only chart you're responsible for today is Day 3 of your 7-Day Food Diary. The most important activity at hand is reading and learning, so sit back, open your mind, and enjoy.

Stocking Up on Motivation

On page 54 you'll find Day 3 of your 7-Day Food Diary. How do you feel about filling it out today? Answer honestly.

(Your answer) _____

If you're like most people, you're probably starting to find it a bit of a bore. Technically, the task—writing down the foods you eat—is the same today as it was yesterday and the day before. Psychologically, however, it's a different story. Keeping a food diary may seem not only an infringement on your valuable time but an altogether unreasonable and petty request. Why does the task seem suddenly more difficult?

Lack of motivation.

Think of your motivation as a glowing fire. It was burning brightly on Day 1 and was still going strong on Day 2. But today, on Day 3, it's starting to dim.

Other diet books and methods treat motivation as a kind of eternal flame. Once lit, it will burn indefinitely of its own accord. I don't adhere to this magical theory. I believe that the fire of motivation must be constantly attended to. This belief is what makes the 10-day diet countdown different from other methods you have tried before. This time, instead of taking motivation for granted, we will work together to strengthen it. And this time, no matter how many times you have failed in the past, you will succeed.

So let's take a minute right now to refuel.

What was the motivation that brought you to this book in the first place? You wanted to lose weight, of course. But you don't need me to tell you how to do that. You already know that weight loss depends on eating less and moving more. People come to me because they have trouble putting this simple principle into practice. They are depressed, guilty, unhappy, and frightened. *They feel their eating has slipped out of control.*

You may think being slim is one of the cornerstones of happiness, but a much more important cornerstone is the psychological need each of us has to feel in control of his or her life. If you have ever binged on food, you know exactly what I am talking about. Feelings of helplessness, isolation, and self-disgust probably gripped you and left you feeling cut off from the rest of the world and unable to take part in its pleasures.

You picked up this book because you wanted to gain control of your eating habits. And you still want that, don't you?

(Your answer) _____

Think for a moment how it would feel to be in charge of your diet.

Imagine choosing foods that are nutritious and right for your body instead of stuffing yourself on foods you know are "poisonous." Imagine a life so full that turning down a piece of pizza would be no more important to you than turning off a light switch. It's a tantalizing, liberating image, isn't it?

Now, the big question: To achieve this kind of control, are you willing to continue keeping your 7-Day Food Diary?

(Your answer) _____

You may not realize it, but keeping a food diary isn't just an intelligence-gathering exercise, although the information it yields will certainly be helpful. The process of keeping the diary is valuable in itself.

Every time you write down what you eat, you:

- *Reaffirm* your decision to change your behavior pattern.
- *Reinforce* your commitment to lose weight.
- *Learn* to associate food with positive rational action rather than mindless impulse.
- *Prove* to yourself that you can follow through with your commitment.
- *Become aware* of each and every time food enters your body.

By keeping your 7-Day Food Diary you are, whether you realize it or not, taking charge of your eating patterns!

This morning, at the beginning of Day 3, you are closer to gaining control of your eating habits than you were on Day 1. And by tonight, after you have completed Day 3 of the food diary, you will be closer still.

How is your motivation now? Refueled and roaring? If it isn't, read this section one more time, letting every word sink in. Then go on to Day 3 of your food diary.

7-DAY FOOD DIARY

For each entry, include the food you ate as well as all beverages, the time and circumstances, and any important feelings you had.

DAY 3

Day _____ Date _____

Breakfast _____

_____

Between _____

_____

Lunch _____

_____

Between _____

_____

Dinner _____

_____

Between_____

_____

Thoughts _____

_____

_____

What's Changed?

You are still eight days away from Take-Off Day. You are free to eat anything and everything you want. In the past, you may have looked upon this time as the last oasis before crossing the diet desert—your last chance to "enjoy yourself." It isn't at all uncommon for people to go on one last, wild, pound-producing binge before starting a diet.

Is that what's happening to you this time? If you're keeping your food diary, it probably isn't. A very large number of my patients report that the simple act of writing down what they eat automatically and painlessly reduces their intake.

Why?

Many of us eat mindlessly, without thinking about what we're consuming, without asking ourselves if we really want it or not. Keeping a food diary involves mental effort. It brings the mind into play and, once this happens, the mind begins to exert its own sensible influence. Your taste buds may want an entire container of berries-and-cheesecake ice cream, but your mind doesn't. When your mind is part of the decision-making process, compromise is likely: a scoop of berries-and-cheesecake ice cream instead of a whole container or, better yet, a simple bowl of fresh berries. It's just this kind of negotiation and compromise that takes place, on a subconscious level, when you keep a food diary.

Why not make your 7-Day Food Diary a Rest-of-Your-Life Food Diary then?

Because it just isn't practical. However effective a food diary may be in helping you to eat less, the idea of keeping one forever is a motivation burner, not a motivation builder, and in this book I have promised that you will find nothing but motivation builders.

Early in my career I began searching for a technique that, like the food diary, would give the mind a chance to approve—or veto—food choices. It seemed that such a technique would be vital in helping my patients achieve and maintain weight loss. After all, offering the overweight person a diet without teaching her how to follow it is like giving someone a sports car without teaching her to drive. The result is bound to be a smashup.

I wanted to develop a technique that would allow the dieter to tap into his motivation and use that powerful motivation as a tool. The technique had to be practical, easy to learn, easy to remember, and easy to use. It had to be a technique that could be implemented anytime, anywhere, and in any circumstances.

The result of my search was what I call the Touch-Control Method.

I want you to learn this method because it will mark the difference between your success and failure. Simple though it is, it has allowed hundreds of people—people who have tried and failed to control their eating many times before—to achieve and maintain weight loss.

Are you ready to learn the Touch-Control Method?

(Your answer) _____

Attention Skeptics

Was your answer to the last question hesitant? I'm not surprised. Another "magical" weight-loss method, you may be thinking. Another program that doesn't deliver what it promises.

Most overweight people have failed to lose weight so many times they've become jaded to the very possibility of success. Take a moment now to write down why you don't think my technique will work for you. Really let loose with your criticism! This is a good place to express your anger at all the other diet systems that have failed to work for you.

_____

_____

_____

_____

_____

_____

_____

_____

_____

_____

_____

Unless you wrote down something like, "Because I have no intention of beginning a diet on Take-Off Day," the Touch-Control Method *will* work for you. It will work because it uses the most powerful dieting tool there is: your own motivation.

"Oh sure," you say sarcastically. "I've got *tons* of motivation—that's why I'm in this fix."

Most dieters have been brainwashed into thinking they have no motivation to draw on. The negative, self-deprecating messages are everywhere: in television commercials that show a decidedly overweight actor arranging immense plates of cold cuts and good-naturedly wondering if the feast will be "enough"; in slogans such as "Fat is just desserts"; in "cute" refrigerator magnets that proclaim "Willpower? I ate mine."

Fortunately, having worked with hundreds of overweight people, I know that motivation isn't the problem. My patients are often people of tremendous drive and considerable achievement. You already have all the motivation you need. The trick is to focus it on the task at hand.

Does this scenario sound familiar? You're on a diet. You've resolved not to overeat. But, suddenly, you're face to face with a "forbidden" food item. Your impulse is to grab it. But you know you really shouldn't. A tiny voice whispers the word *no* in the back of your mind. You've promised yourself you won't overeat. You don't really want to. Or do you? Suddenly, the desire to eat is all you can feel, all you can think about. This desire takes over and before you know what's happening, the food is in your mouth—and you're left feeling like a failure once again. The guilt alone is enough to make you want to eat more.

What happened here? It's really very simple. You let go of the rope marked *Motivation* and grabbed a rope marked *Craving*. Both ropes are strong. They have a powerful pull and will lead you in quite different directions. The Touch-Control Method is going to strengthen your hold on the rope marked *Motivation*. When your hands are tightly holding that rope, it will be easier to leave the rope marked *Craving* dangling in the wind.

My Touch-Control Method isn't magical. As good as this tool is, it won't work by itself. Unless you make a conscious decision to alter your eating habits, you won't lose any weight at all. But you've already made that difficult decision, haven't you? Take a moment now to reaffirm commitment and your reasons for making it. Use the space below for your answer.

_____

_____

_____

_____

_____

This time, you're going to succeed. Because when the Touch-Control Method is combined with a healthful, low-calorie diet and a reasonable program of exercise, weight loss is inevitable.

Are you less skeptical now?

(Your answer) _____

Good. You're ready to learn.

THE TOUCH-CONTROL METHOD

Take a few minutes to complete this simple quiz.

1. Right now I feel:

_____	Hungry	_____	Energetic
_____	Angry	_____	Relaxed
_____	Lonely	_____	Refreshed
_____	Tired	_____	Confident
_____	Stressed	_____	Happy
_____	Bored	_____	Other: _____
_____	Worried	_____	Other: _____

2. Right now, on a 1 to 10 scale (with 1 being the lowest and 10 the highest), thoughts of food rate a number _____ in my mind.

    1   2   3   4   5   6   7   8   9   10

3. These are the foods I'm thinking of:

_____

_____

_____

_____

_____

4. These are the other things on my mind:

_____

_____

_____

_____

_____

Now let's learn the Touch-Control Method. It's very simple. Just follow these four basic steps:

The Touch-Control Method

- *Step 1.* Look upward and while looking up, close your eyes slowly.
- *Step 2.* Now take a deep breath and exhale gently. With the tip of your forefinger, touch any part of your face: your cheek, your temple, the area around your mouth, or any other place that is comfortable for you.
- *Step 3.* Repeat the following three Stoplines to yourself.

For my body, overeating is an insult and a poison.

I need my body to live.

I owe my body this respect and attention.

- *Step 4.* Take another deep, unhurried breath, exhale, and open your eyelids.
- *Step 5.* Now shift your awareness towards your stomach and become aware of how it feels: hungry? comfortable? full?
- *Step 6.* Look at the food in front of you and clinically evaluate if it is the right *kind* of food and the right *amount* of food for your body.

The whole process should take only about twenty seconds. After you have performed it once, pause. Go back and perform the Touch-Control Method again. Take a few more breaths before performing it a third and final time.

The Touch-Control Method should become like an automatic reflex, working to help you resist the foods you don't want your body to have. This simple technique will keep you in touch with your feelings of hunger or satiety. It will put an end to your automatic, "unconscious" reaching out for food by putting a ten- to twenty-second time break between you and the food in front of you. This is just the time necessary to prevent yourself from destructive overeating.

When you have finished practicing the Touch-Control Method, take the same test you took a few minutes ago:

1. Right now I feel:

_____ Hungry   _____ Energetic

_____ Angry   _____ Relaxed

_____ Lonely   _____ Refreshed

_____ Tired   _____ Confident

_____ Stressed   _____ Happy

_____ Bored   _____ Other: _____

_____ Worried   _____ Other: _____

2. Right now, on a 1 to 10 scale (with 1 being the lowest and 10 the highest), thoughts of food rate a number _____ in my mind.

      1   2   3   4   5   6   7   8   9   10

3. These are the foods I'm thinking of:

_____

_____

_____

_____

_____

4. These are the other things on my mind:

_____

_____

_____

_____

Compare your answers on these two identical tests. Did your mental state undergo a change?

Most people find that the Touch-Control Method is truly a mind-altering experience. If you were preoccupied with doubts, worries, and thoughts of food, you probably saw a dramatic change in your outlook. (If you were initially in a relaxed and nonhungry state, the change may be imperceptible. Come back and try the experiment again later.)

As amazing as it is, the method isn't permanent in its effect. Once is not enough. If your thoughts of food initially rated high on the scale, you may find those same thoughts coming back again sooner or later. This isn't a problem. The Touch-Control Method is inexhaustible and takes so little time you can use it over and over again. Just go back and repeat the process each time you need it. Feel yourself relaxing, tapping into your motivation, and reaffirming your decision not to eat.

Now, for the first time in your life, you have a real and effective weapon to use whenever a food craving threatens to overwhelm your resolve. With this weapon you will succeed in your diet, even if you have failed before.

"It's so simple," said a patient named Mitzi. "I don't see how it can possibly work."

But Mitzi herself was proof that the method *does* work. Mitzi was a classic roller-coaster dieter, someone who had started out at a hefty 160 pounds and "dieted" her way up to an obese 220. Now she was a healthy 133, a weight she had been successfully maintaining for over a year.

"The important thing," I pointed out to her, "is that the technique works. So does it really matter how?"

"I guess I'm just naturally curious," Mitzi said. "I'd like to know."

There's no particular reason why you need to understand how the Touch-Control Method works. It will be just as successful for you if you never learn another thing about it. But if you're the curious type like Mitzi, here's what happens each time you perform the six basic steps.

When you glance upward and briefly close your eyes, you are clearing your mind of clutter and destructive impulses and focusing yourself on what you really want.

When you gently bring your finger to your face, you are warning and warming yourself in a primal, time-honored way. Nothing is as comforting as a touch, and nothing is as certain to get your attention. The best part is that you can give yourself this powerful boost without anyone else being aware of what you are doing.

When you say, "For my body, overeating is an insult and a poison," you are directing your thoughts away from the seductive taste of food and focusing them instead on the destructive effects of overeating. Your natural protective instincts are coming into your awareness.

When you say, "I need my body to live," you are restating your priorities in the simplest and most direct terms. You are tapping into your motivation, and this allows you to resist temptation.

When you say, "I owe my body this respect and attention," you are reaffirming the most powerful weapon of all: the love you have for yourself and the love you have for your body, which is the physical extension of your self.

When you breathe deeply, you relax. When you are truly relaxed, it's impossible to feel anxious. A feeling of well-being and calm will make it even easier for you to resist the urge to eat. You have gained valuable time, and you will feel the urge to eat dissipate. It has passed and once again you feel in control of your eating.

Now that you've learned the Touch-Control Method, I want you to do one more thing. Make it your own by putting the three Stoplines in your own handwriting. Write them on a three-by-five-inch index card and keep this card with you throughout your diet. Look at it often, even after you know the Stoplines by heart and are a pro at using the Touch-Control Method. Seeing the words in your own writing will further reinforce your motivation to stick with your decision to diet.

Before You Go . . .

Before you go on with your day today, there's one more thing I want you to see in your own writing: a word of praise. I have noticed that people often have a hard time accepting compliments, even when they are highly deserved. Often, patients of mine will feel so uncomfortable with the compliments they receive as they lose weight that they find themselves returning to their old eating habits.

"Why should I be praised for being normal?" they reason. "I really don't deserve all of this."

I want you to begin getting comfortable with the idea that you do deserve praise. Dieting is not easy and it's not something anyone else can do for you. The techniques you are learning in this book are helpful, but they are only techniques, useless unless *you* put them to work.

Use the space on the next page to honor your motivation and your commitment to your goal. Words such as "I am now fully committed to my goal of losing _____ pounds and am moving closer to that goal every day" are totally appropriate, but don't limit yourself—lavish as much praise on yourself as you like!

_____

_____

_____

_____

_____

_____

_____

_____

DAY FOUR

CONFRONT YOUR RESISTANCE DAY

Today's the day to:

- Practice the Touch-Control Method.
- Complete Day 4 of your 7-Day Food Diary.
- Target your resistance points.
- Convert resistance points to bonus points.

Practicing the Touch-Control Method

TODAY, THE first time you are tempted to overeat, I would like you to practice the Touch-Control Method. I would like you to practice it at least once, but the more times you practice it successfully, the better off you will be.

You aren't on a diet yet, so why am I asking you to do this?

The answer is very simple. Human beings are creatures of habit. Whatever you did in a given situation in the past, you are likely to do in a similar situation in the future.

Most diet programs fail to take this into account. They do nothing to prepare the dieter beforehand. Thus, when a situation involving food arises, the dieter finds himself in a state of crisis. His motivation is telling him to stick with the diet but his old behavior patterns are telling him to *eat, eat, eat!*

Is it any wonder that so many diets fail?

Your diet will not fail because day by day, assignment by assignment, the 10-day diet countdown is preparing you for the situations, stresses, and temptations that are part of any dieting effort. By the time you reach Take-Off Day, you will know what to do *instead* of reverting to your old behavior patterns.

At first you may feel uncomfortable or even self-conscious practicing the Touch-Control Method. That's only natural. After all, it's new to you. But as you practice it more and more often, the newness will wear off and it will seem like the right and appropriate thing to do.

Remember . . .

Each time you are tempted to overeat and do, you are reinforcing the behavior pattern that made you fat.

Each time you are tempted to overeat and instead use the Touch-Control Method, you are establishing a new, healthier behavior pattern.

The more often you practice the method, the more natural it will seem to you. Gradually, it will become a habit, replacing the old habit of overeating.

On the next page you'll find Day 4 of your 7-Day Food Diary. As you fill it in today, note the times you practiced the Touch-Control Method and how easy or difficult you found it.

7-DAY FOOD DIARY

For each entry, include the food you ate as well as any beverage, the time and circumstances, and any important feelings you had.

DAY 4

Day _____ Date _____

Breakfast _____

_____

Between _____

_____

Lunch _____

_____

Between _____

_____

Dinner _____

_____

Between _____

_____

Thoughts _____

_____

_____

Resistance: The Last Frontier

Read the following brief case histories.

Cindy, thirty-three, had been dieting most of her life in an attempt to compete with her slim mother and gorgeous older sister. She had just begun another weight-loss program when the opportunity came to fly home for a family re-union. She told her family she was dieting, and her mother and sister both were very supportive. At the picnic, however, they seemed to spend most of their time offering Cindy potato salad, chips, dip, cake, and ice cream. At first Cindy refused, but eventually she agreed with her loved ones that "just a taste couldn't hurt." This was the beginning of the end for Cindy's diet. By the time she came to see me, she was twenty pounds heavier than she had been at the time of that trip home.

Paul came to me as an obese young man who had never, in his twenty-four years, dated. "Girls don't find me attractive," he said. "But I find *them* attractive, so I'm going to lose this weight." I was sure that someone so well-motivated would be an ideal patient and for several months Paul was. It was truly wonderful to watch him shed his reclusive ways and begin enjoying himself with others. "Just a few more pounds," he joked, "and I'll be ready for a real relationship." Then the unexpected happened. Paul began to binge. It took several sessions before, together, we unraveled what the problem was.

Nell, in her mid forties, was one of the few black women of her time to receive a law degree from a prestigious Ivy League school. On the surface she was calm, precise, and extremely articulate. She was also anxious to lose twenty pounds. But, almost from the start, she found dieting uncomfortable and difficult. "It isn't physical," she explained in her clear-thinking way. "It's in my mind. Part of me wants to drop this weight but another part of me keeps reaching for food. It isn't that I want to be fat—it's that I want to eat!"

What do these three different people have in common? They have all encountered *resistance.*

Speaking in a general way, the dictionary tells us that resistance is "the opposition offered by one force to another." From a psychological point of view, resistance is a phenomenon unto itself. No matter how sincerely or ardently one desires change, there is always a part of the self that doesn't want to change, that is comfortable with the old way of doing things, that is going to fight tooth and nail to keep the status quo. No true or permanent change can come about until the resistance point, whatever it is, is met, challenged, and overcome.

Ordinarily, I do not encourage people to play armchair psychologist—it can be an extremely dangerous game! But, just for today, I'm going to lift the ban.

If this exercise doesn't appeal to you, consider it optional. Go right on to page 73 and continue reading. However, looking at other people's problems can sometimes be helpful. First, it can get the spotlight off you for a while and help you realize you are neither unique nor alone. Secondly, it can help you develop an objective eye that may help you tackle—and solve—your own problems.

Look closely at the situations Cindy, Paul, and Nell found themselves in. What can you say about their resistance points? Can you guess what brought those resistance points into play? Of course, you don't have nearly as much information as you need to make an accurate guess, but for the moment that doesn't matter. I just want you to explore the possibilities in each scenario and jot down your thoughts.

Cindy

_____

_____

_____

_____

_____

_____

_____

Paul

_____

_____

_____

_____

_____

_____

Nell

_____

_____

_____

_____

_____

_____

_____

Now that you have written down your thoughts, let's explore together what made reaching their goals so difficult for these people.

Cindy had always been the family ugly duckling. Although her mother and sister wanted her to be slim and lovely, as they were, they also had a subconscious desire for her to remain fat. Cindy, poor homely little thing, allowed them unlimited opportunities to feel superior. The thought of a slim Cindy was unsettling to them and so they offered her all sorts of food. Subconsciously, Cindy knew very well that her mother and sister were sending out mixed signals. She knew that becoming slim would upset the family applecart. Cindy could have overcome this block to her motivation but she didn't. Instead she silently agreed to continue her role as ugly duckling and sealed the bargain with a plate of potato salad.

Paul had put his life on hold early. At the age of eight he dropped out of Little League because he was self-conscious about his weight. "I knew I would lose that baby fat soon," he explained. "After all, my mother kept telling me I would—and when I did, I would join up again and become the team's star." Little League was just the beginning. As adolescence dawned, Paul found himself putting off more and more life experiences: learning to dance, going to parties, dating girls. "I always told myself I'd do this or do that when I lost weight," Paul explained. For Paul, as for most of us, life experiences are fraught with anxiety as well as excitement. Although Paul liked girls, he was nervous about forming a relationship. Instead of dealing with his ambiguous feelings directly, Paul hid behind a security blanket of fat. As the blanket started to slide away, Paul's fears of rejection surfaced.

Nell had succeeded against the odds, climbing to success in a white male world. She had paid a price along the way, though. Hearing her story, I was shocked and dismayed at the many incidents of prejudice she had had to endure. Nell claimed to carry no scars and harbor no anger. "It's part of the game," she said. "You can ignore the good old boys and eventually they'll leave you alone. Or you can fight them and be destroyed." Nell's survival depended on her ability to suppress her anger. She credited her courtroom success with her ability to be, as she put it, "100 percent rational, a kind of legalistic machine.'' Nell's food diary told a different story. Nell wasn't a legalistic machine by nature. Whenever a situation arose in which she felt she could not vent her emotions—particularly anger—she reached for food. Nell was, literally, stuffing down her feelings with excess calories.

As these three case histories suggest, resistance has many different causes; the result, however, is always the same: It makes achieving a set goal difficult and sometimes, depending on how strong the resistance is, impossible.

What makes resistance so powerful? Its mysterious nature. By ''mysterious'' I mean that the person who is experiencing such a block cannot see the block clearly, and this makes it seem overwhelming to him. It's as if you were walking blindfolded down a path and suddenly bumped into a barrier. With the blindfold on, the barrier seems gigantic: It emits a thunderous noise and so you assume it is a hundred stories tall, a hundred miles wide. You take a step backward, then march forward again—only to bump once again into the barrier. There is no limit to how many times this can happen.

Resistance works in much the same way. Cindy, Paul, and Nell all bumped repeatedly into a nameless desire to eat. But after they discovered the source of their resistance, each person was able to see the problem clearly and decide what to do about it. When this happened, the desire to eat subsided.

How do you know you are up against your own resistance? Here are some possible clues:

- Feeling anxious or uncomfortable
- Feeling despair—as if ''you'll never make it,'' even though your goal is closer than ever before
- Feeling angry
- Feeling sad
- Feeling rebellious, as if your goal had been set by others and not by yourself
- Feeling a sense of loss

- Feeling frightened
- Losing energy
- Losing interest in your goal
- Returning to your destructive habits

Now take a few minutes to complete the Resistance Inventory on the next page. (It's possible that, because you are still counting down to Take-Off Day your resistance hasn't surfaced yet. If this is the case and you answer no to question 1 on the next page, put this quiz aside until it is meaningful to you.)

RESISTANCE INVENTORY

1. Read again through the clues to resistance in the list on pages 74 and 75. Have you identified any of them within yourself? List which ones:

   _____

   _____

   _____

   _____

   _____

2. Do you have any other feelings which you think are caused by resistance? Describe:

   _____

   _____

   _____

   _____

3. On a 1 to 10 scale, how strong are these feelings?
Anxiety/discomfort:

| 1 | 2 | 3 | 4 | 5 | 6 | 7 | 8 | 9 | 10 |

Despair:

| 1 | 2 | 3 | 4 | 5 | 6 | 7 | 8 | 9 | 10 |

Anger:

| 1 | 2 | 3 | 4 | 5 | 6 | 7 | 8 | 9 | 10 |

Sadness:

| 1 | 2 | 3 | 4 | 5 | 6 | 7 | 8 | 9 | 10 |

Rebelliousness:

    1   2   3   4   5   6   7   8   9   10

Sense of Loss:

    1   2   3   4   5   6   7   8   9   10

Fright:

    1   2   3   4   5   6   7   8   9   10

Loss of energy:

    1   2   3   4   5   6   7   8   9   10

Loss of interest:

    1   2   3   4   5   6   7   8   9   10

Return to destructive habits:

    1   2   3   4   5   6   7   8   9   10

Other: _____

    1   2   3   4   5   6   7   8   9   10

Other: _____

    1   2   3   4   5   6   7   8   9   10

Other: _____

    1   2   3   4   5   6   7   8   9   10

4. When are these feelings most likely to occur?

_____

_____

_____

_____

_____

_____

The Flower Garden of Resistance

As I said before, there are many different causes of resistance. Because each person is a unique individual with a different life story, no two cases are exactly alike. However, generalizations can be made.

A number of common causes of resistance are described below. You will undoubtedly notice that some of them overlap and some could be grouped together under one category, yet each is just a little different from the others. I arranged them this way on purpose, so that you could see how many and varied the causes of resistance are.

You will also notice that many of these causes contain flawed and even irrational thinking. That's because resistance usually does not involve conscious thought but is a complex spider web of subconscious fears and beliefs.

As you read, notice which of the causes trigger thoughts and feelings of your own. If you find yourself reacting to or identifying with one of the causes, stop reading. Give yourself a moment to let your thoughts unwind. You may be on your way to discovering one of your own resistance points. Don't let these important awarenesses slip away from you. Turn to page 83 and jot down your thoughts before continuing to read.

You resist because losing weight means losing your physical self. Each of us has a concept of our physical being. Even if you are not pleased with your body, it is still *your* body, and even a change for the better can be disruptive. I have often had patients tell me that losing weight made them feel vulnerable. One young woman, seeing her collarbones emerge for the first time, became inordinately fearful of breaking one of them. This was true even though she claimed to be delighted with her "new" body.

You resist because losing weight means losing your personality. Does overweight play a part in the role you have created for yourself? Are you the kind of big, cuddly guy who's every woman's big brother? Are you the tart-tongued *Roseanne* of your neighborhood? If overweight plays a part in the role you have created for yourself, losing weight can be a threatening proposition. Subconsciously, you may fear that it will mean giving up your identity.

You resist because losing weight goes against leftover messages from childhood. As we were growing up, all of us received certain messages about ourselves. Some of those messages had to do with food and our bodies, and today—twenty, thirty, or even forty years later—those messages still play in our subconscious. Some of the messages may have been positive, such as "It's good to clean your plate," or "Being big is being powerful," or "Food will make you strong." Some of them may have been negative, like "I guess little Dot will always be a fatty." Positive or negative, the message went into your subconscious and became a rule to live by.

You resist because losing weight goes against the wishes of others. Sometimes even people who love us have a subconscious desire to keep us fat. This was certainly the case with Cindy, wasn't it? Other variations include the husband who bemoans his wife's weight but fears what will happen if she becomes attractive to other men, and the chum who fears the competition her newly thin friend will give her. When people around us have a subconscious desire to keep us fat, they send out mixed signals. The dieter picks up the signals, interprets the meaning, and conspires to preserve the status quo by failing at yet another diet.

You resist because losing weight means gaining the approval of others. Perverse, isn't it? Why on earth should gaining approval be a block? Sometimes there are leftover childhood messages at work, such as "You're a bad girl," "You don't deserve the approval of others," or "You'll never succeed." Or there can be an internal fear that goes something like this: "If I enjoy approval, everyone will think I need approval; and if everyone thinks I need approval, they will see me as desperate and pathetic. I'm better off pretending approval doesn't matter to me at all!" Some people fear that doing what pleases others will mean losing their individuality and becoming "just like everyone else." Others don't like approval because it suggests that they have been "wrong" while others have been "right." Still others sniff at approval based on anything as trivial as weight loss. "If my friends really loved me," they storm, "they would love me no matter what!" Finally, the dieter may be so angry at those who have been nagging him about his weight that he refuses to do anything that might give them pleasure.

You resist because dieting means losing control. For some people, food represents the ultimate control. Your spouse may make demands, your children may have expectations, your boss may have unrealistic goals, and the clock is always, always against you. You dance to the tune of a hundred pipers and feel forever overwhelmed, put upon, and on the verge of collapse. The one domain you exercise complete authority over is the food you eat. If you agree to follow a set diet, even this small measure of authority will slip from your hands.

You resist because losing weight means losing your excuses. Remember Paul, the young man who wanted to lose weight and begin a social life? Paul is typical of a great many people who use fat as a reason to avoid the uncomfortable and hazard-fraught challenges of life. Such people have convinced themselves that they would become smart, rich, happy, and successful *if only* they could lose weight. But they don't really believe it. How can they, when there are so many overweight people who have achieved these very things without losing a single pound? People such as Paul resist losing weight because staying fat is easier than embarking on the risky path to achievement.

You resist because you have mixed feelings about yourself as a sexual being. This may have been part of Paul's resistance, too. Although an occasional cause of resistance among men, it is far more common among women. Why? Because women are more often raised with the notion that nice girls don't—or, at the very least, shouldn't want to. Being sexy can represent anything from being a bad girl to being a vulnerable one, and some people find it easier to bypass sexuality altogether. Not only is food an acceptable substitute for physical intimacy, but carrying extra weight around can actually lower one's natural sex drive.

You resist because food or overweight protects you from your emotions. Nell, the brilliant black lawyer, used food to stuff down the anger. As long as she was eating, she was distracting herself from feelings she didn't know how to cope with. Other people use not food but weight to keep them from dealing with emotions head on. I'll never forget the patient who discovered the cause of her resistance when I asked her what would happen if she lost weight. "If I lost weight and was attractive," she blurted out, "I'd cheat on my husband just like he cheated on me ten years ago!" Since this patient also loved her husband very much, she had used her weight as insurance against acting out her buried anger.

You resist because overweight is your screening mechanism. No doubt about it, there are a lot of frauds and charlatans in the world, and a lot of ways of being hurt. Some people carry extra weight around in an attempt to buffer themselves from these harsh realities. They harbor the belief that "good" people—those capable of loving someone for what she is, not how she looks—will approach despite the barrier of weight, while bad and insincere people will turn back.

You resist because giving up food means giving up excitement. You may have become so focused on food that each meal has to be a party and each evening has to be enlivened with a hot fudge fiesta. If food has taken the place ordinarily occupied by friends, family, romance, hobbies, books, music, movies, and other entertainments, the notion of giving it up is bound to leave you with a feeling of emptiness.

You resist because giving up food means giving up a way of coping with stress. Eating may be your way of loosening up and relaxing, and many heavy people routinely reach for food to relieve stress. Eating can distract you from whatever's bothering you. It can also soothe you, make you feel loved, remind you of happier times, and give you the illusion of control. Of course, the effect is only temporary but the subconscious does not see this. It persists in the belief that eating will make you feel better.

You resist because giving up food means giving up an avoidance mechanism. What would you rather do: scrub a floor or eat a brownie? Many people avoid life's tedious little tasks by keeping themselves perpetually busy with the preparation and consumption of food. Often, these are people with a strong work ethic. They'd feel guilty reading a book when the washing needs to be done and even guiltier watching television when they planned to wax the car. But because eating is a necessity, they can feel justifiably productive while still procrastinating any number of tasks.

You resist because you are in a state of denial. You don't really believe you have a serious problem. Eating less would be nice and being thinner would be nice, but it isn't really that important. To prove your point, you refuse to take the diet seriously. Taking it seriously, after all, would mean that you really do have a problem, and that's something you're not about to admit.

You resist because you aren't firmly committed to your goal. Losing weight is hard work—work that requires a firm commitment. If you decide to lose weight to appear slim at your class reunion, to make your partner proud of you, to conform to company standards, or for some other reason rooted in the outside world instead of in your own consciousness, your commitment may not be strong enough.

Targeting Your Resistance Points

Did any of these causes strike a familiar chord in you? Uncovering the causes of one's own resistance isn't easy. It means taking a good, hard look in the mirror and seeing oneself, warts and all. Would you be willing to do that to help achieve your goal?

(Your answer) _____

The important thing to remember is that losing weight—not maintaining your present weight—is your real goal. That's why you bought this book. That's why you've worked so hard to get where you are right now. Resistance is just a roadblock that gets in your way.

The first step to getting around that roadblock is to target your resistance points. Use the next few pages to do just that. If you need to, go back and read about the different causes of resistance again, asking which do and don't apply to yourself. Another way to uncover your resistance is to ask yourself what would be the worst thing that could happen if you gave up overeating or became slim. Even if your mind seems blank, you should spend the next ten minutes (or longer, if you like) writing about resistance. Be honest. Let your barriers down. Let your higher self lead the way.

Resistance Notebook

This place is for you to write about the fears, false assumptions, and mythic beliefs that block your path to achievement. Come back to it as often as you like and write as much as you wish. This is your private place and no one else's!

_____

_____

_____

_____

_____

_____

_____

_____

_____

_____

_____

_____
_____
_____
_____
_____
_____
_____
_____
_____
_____
_____
_____
_____
_____
_____
_____
_____
_____
_____
_____
_____

Converting Resistance Points to Bonus Points

How can you change resistance points that block success into bonus points that speed it along? The process is twofold.

First, *keep motivation strong by focusing on your true and chosen goal: losing weight.* Already, you have learned some techniques (such as the Touch-Control Method) that will help you do this. In the days to come, you'll be learning more motivation-building skills.

Second, *resolve each resistance point as it arises.* This isn't as hard as it sounds. You can resolve almost any resistance point by using this simple three-step process on it:

- *Step 1.* Identify the resistance point. What is the underlying fear, need, or false belief that is causing your resistance?
- *Step 2.* Evaluate the resistance point. Is it simply a false belief, like the belief that overeating is a good way to cope with stress? Or is your fear based in reality, like Cindy's fear that losing weight would cause friction in her family?
- *Step 3.* Decide what to do. If the resistance point is rooted in a false belief, discard it in favor of a belief that is valid, such as "Overeating is not a good way to cope with stress, but taking a long walk is." If the resistance point is based in reality, decide how you will deal with the problem. Cindy might have reached a decision such as, "Losing weight is important to me. If it causes friction with my mother and sister, I will confront those problems when they arise."

Below are some spaces for you to resolve your own resistance points. Be sure to resolve each different resistance point as it becomes clear to you.

My resistance point is: _____

_____

_____

_____

I have thought about whether my resistance is based on a false belief or in reality, and this is my evaluation:

_____

_____

_____

This is what I have decided to do: _____

_____

_____

_____

My resistance point is: _____

_____

_____

_____

I have thought about whether my resistance is based on a false belief or in reality, and this is my evaluation:

_____

_____

_____

This is what I have decided to do: _____

_____

_____

_____

My resistance point is: _____

_____

_____

_____

I have thought about whether my resistance is based on a false belief or in reality, and this is my evaluation:

_____

_____

_____

This is what I have decided to do: _____

_____

_____

_____

Now It's Your Turn for a Bonus!

You've done something very difficult, something many people never find the courage to do. You've been willing to look at yourself with unflinching honesty! The real reward, of course, will come when you begin your diet and discover that your hard work has armed you with the tools you need to reach your goal.

In the meantime, you deserve a bonus! Think of something (within reason) that would make you happy and treat yourself to it. Maybe it's a call to a friend, relaxing with a crossword puzzle, buying something new, or splurging on fresh raspberries in December.

Don't just yawn and go on about your day's business. *Rewarding yourself is important because it reinforces your motivation.* So right now, decide what your reward will be and when you will enjoy it.

This is the reward I have chosen for myself today:

_____

_____

This is when I will enjoy it:

_____

_____

DAY
FIVE

MOTIVATION MUSCLE DAY

Today's the day to:
- Fill in Day 5 of your 7-Day Food Diary.
- Begin thinking of yourself as a thin eater.
- Build motivation and blast stress through self-hypnosis.

SIT BACK, relax! You put in a hard day yesterday confronting your own resistance. Today is going to be much easier. Today you will painlessly learn about self-hypnosis, a relaxation technique that will help you resist the temptation to overeat.

On the next page you will find Day 5 of your 7-Day Food Diary. Continue to fill it in just as you have done on previous days. I know it may seem routine by now, and perhaps you think you have already gathered all the information you need, but please continue with this undertaking. It is the hardest thing you will be asked to do today.

7-DAY FOOD DIARY

For each entry, include the food you ate as well as all beverages, the time and circumstances, and any important feelings you had.

DAY 5

Day _____ Date _____

Breakfast _____

_____

Between _____

_____

Lunch _____

_____

Between _____

_____

Dinner _____

_____

Between _____

_____

Thoughts _____

_____

_____

Thin versus Fat Eating

Many patients say they have been told to "think thin" so often they want to scream. I don't blame them. To me, telling someone to "think thin" is absolutely useless. As I said earlier, it's like telling a lifelong landlubber to jump off the high board.

Some people seem to be born thinking thin. Others are lucky enough to develop a thin eating pattern as they grow up. But, for a variety of reasons, many of us develop patterns that are exactly the opposite. To achieve and maintain your desired weight, you will have to change your eating style. That's a challenge, of course, just as changing any ingrained habit is. But it isn't impossible. Today, together, we are going to start making the switch.

Are you ready to begin that process?

(Your answer) _____

To turn from fat to thin eating, you must first know the differences between the two. Perhaps you think you already know what those differences are, but don't be too certain. While you may be aware of some kinds of fat eating, your own bad habits—the very ones that cause you to gain weight—may be invisible to you.

Once, a somewhat overweight friend of mine sat in my kitchen nibbling from a container of strawberries. "It must be awful to cram down thousands of calories of bread and jam in one sitting," she commented. "What makes people eat such disgustingly fattening food?"

Midway through the strawberries, my friend began to feel full. That didn't slow her down, though. "These strawberries are so delicious," she said, then went on to comment on a friend of hers with a disastrous penchant for cream cheese.

Finally, my friend looked at the nearly empty container of berries. "I'm stuffed," she said, "but since there're only a few berries left, I hate to see them go to waste." And she popped them into her mouth.

My friend is convinced she doesn't have an eating problem. "Just a little middle-age spread" is the term she uses to describe her weight. She believes—wrongly—that stuffing oneself on low-calorie foods is harmless. Well, it is something everyone has done at one time or another. But when it's done routinely, it's a glittering example of fat eating in action.

It isn't the *food* that's eaten but the *rationale* for eating it that makes the difference between fat and thin eating. So, to make you a fully informed eater, let's look at these differences in action.

The "more is better" rationale. Food is fuel for the body. The thin eater eats because her body needs the fuel. This means she takes in food when her inner gauge says "empty" and stops eating when the needle moves to "comfortably full." The fat eater, on the other hand, is focused on the fuel itself. Instead of waiting till his inner gauge says "empty," he takes on fuel whenever it's available to him. Instead of stopping when he is comfortably full, he will often eat until he is so physically uncomfortable he can't take another bite. "If some is good, more is better" may be sound thinking if you're discussing diamonds or shares of IBM, but it's destructive when it comes to food.

The "waste not, want not" rationale. When a thin eater is full he stops eating. Any remaining food becomes either garbage or leftovers. The fat eater secretly believes that letting delicious food go to waste is probably a capital offense, so she lets it go "to waist" instead. She often justifies her overeating by telling herself that a particular food is "irresistible."

The "right time and the right place" rationale. If it's dinnertime and the thin eater isn't hungry, she doesn't eat. If she's at a social function where food abounds and she isn't hungry, she either bypasses the buffet table altogether or takes a token amount, then goes on to enjoy the party. A fat eater eats whenever mealtime comes around, regardless of his hunger level. The idea of skipping a meal makes him profoundly uncomfortable, as if something is out of sync with himself or with the universe. At social gatherings the fat eater feels it's both his right and his duty to eat, whether he's hungry or not. Whether it's to get in a party mood, to make his hostess feel good, or simply to follow the crowd, the fat eater believes that eating is an indispensable part of the event.

The substitution rationale. Each of us has a private list of wants and needs. The thin eater realizes that food will not make his wants and needs go away. The fat eater does not. She may want something (a new job, a relationship, approval, etc.) so much it becomes a deep craving. In her mind, this craving takes on all the trappings of a craving for food. Subconsciously, the fat eater believes she can satisfy the craving by eating. She does not realize that substituting food for the thing she really desires will not satisfy her longing. When she eats and still does not feel content, she meets the crisis by eating more.

Now, do you have an understanding of the differences between fat and thin eating?

(Your answer) _____

Do you think you could recognize fat and thin eating patterns in yourself?

(Your answer) _____

If you answered yes to the last question, congratulations—you are on your way to becoming a thin eater. To help you make the switch, I am going to give you two guiding principles.

Perhaps you think that one of these principles will be *don't overeat,* or something of that sort. Not at all. Telling someone *don't* or *not to* is like waving a red flag at a bull. None of us likes to be told what to do. That's a basic fact of human nature. When you tell yourself, "Don't eat that," you are only daring yourself to eat. This puts you in an immediate trap. Either you don't eat and feel secretly resentful or you rebel, eat the "forbidden" item, and feel like a failure.

Instead of telling you what not to do, the first principle you are going to learn is a positive one: *Always eat with respect for your body.* Think of your body, its value to you, and its needs whenever you eat. This will keep you from treating your body as a garbage can.

The second principle is also positive: *Learn to eat like a gourmet.* Pay complete attention to every mouthful of food that goes into your body: its aroma, appearance, taste, temperature, and texture. Enjoy and savor every bite. If you get pleasure from every mouthful, you won't have to eat more because you "forgot" to taste it fully and feel cheated. You will become satisfied and content while eating less food.

As you work toward making the transition from fat to thin eating, remember that change is not like a light switch. You will not suddenly "turn on" to 100 percent thin eating with no slipups or mistakes. Changing a behavior pattern is a slow and mighty process. Some have compared it to turning the course of a river. So do not become discouraged if, as you begin your diet, you catch yourself repeating old habits. Remember that formerly you were not even in touch with your destructive habits and were making no effort to change them. Now you are aware, and now, meal by meal and mouthful by mouthful, you are in the process of making the change.

Self-Hypnosis, Motivation, and You

Without going into great detail about the theoretical issues of self-hypnosis, I want to alleviate any anxieties you might have about it by simply telling you the fact that there is nothing magical about it. Hypnosis is not sleep, nor are you unconscious, out of control, or under someone else's influence.

The hypnotic trance is a state of alert mental concentration and physical muscle relaxation. While in a hypnotic state you pool your mental energies, bringing your mind to its maximum level of attention and absorption. This process requires your cooperation and participation at all times. It's true that not everybody has the same ability to experience a hypnotic trance state.

However, to a certain degree, everybody can learn to go into this state of physical relaxation and mental alertness.

If you have been hypnotized before, or practiced self-hypnosis, you know exactly what I'm talking about. If you have never experienced this pleasant state, I would like you to think of a particular situation in your life—a situation in which you became totally absorbed in something. Perhaps it was a challenging crafts project, an exciting mystery novel, or a movie or play. Throughout the experience you were totally awake. A ringing phone or an urgent whisper would certainly have caught your attention. Yet, at the same time, you were so completely absorbed that you almost forgot where you were.

This kind of experience, which I am sure you have had, is a form of a hypnotic state. Now that you know what that is, let's go ahead and use it for the purpose of building and keeping your motivation until you have reached your final goal.

Some people think that self-hypnosis means brainwashing yourself with catchphrases like, "I will not eat. I will not eat. I will not eat." How can such a silly technique work? It can't. If you truly want to eat, I can't brainwash you into thinking otherwise. Self-hypnosis is not a magic wand. It cannot give you the desire to do something that you do not truly want to do. However, it can help you to reprogram yourself with new responses to food, eating, and your body.

I already know that you have the motivation it takes to make self-hypnosis work. When you bought this book and set your Take-Off Day, you made a commitment. By working through these first four days, you've proven your motivation beyond the shadow of a doubt.

Your commitment to your goal is bright and shining. It belongs to the very best part of yourself. Motivation is the energy that flows from your positive inner self. To achieve your goal, you need to stay in touch with that inner self. You need to keep your motivation strong and flowing.

Reaching a goal is not always easy. Sometimes there are roadblocks along the way, and these roadblocks can keep you from achieving what you want. Right now, losing weight is your goal. You have decided to diet in order to reach the goal. It seems crystal clear but, in the days to come, clarity may vanish. Different situations, temptations, and pressures may throw you into a state of ''goal confusion.''

How does goal confusion work? Picture a scenario like this: You're at work, busy, and under pressure. An important project is not going right and, to make matters worse, you have just learned that your car needs an expensive tune-up. In five minutes, you're due at a crucial meeting with your boss. When you get home, you will have to make dinner, help your children with their homework, do the dishes, and sort the laundry. If only there were some way to get away from it all, even for a moment. Well, there is; suddenly, you want nothing more than to close your office door and escape into the mindless bliss of a jelly doughnut.

Now you're in a state of goal conflict. Your long-term goal is to diet and lose weight. But your short-term goal is to soothe yourself with food. You want both goals but of course you can't have them. They're diametrically opposed to each other. At this point you begin to bargain with yourself, rationalizing that one little jelly doughnut is not going to hurt. A ''to eat or not to eat'' struggle begins inside you and the struggle produces even more turmoil. You have encountered your own resistance and are stuck. If you eat the doughnut you will feel guilty. If you don't eat it, you will feel deprived and stressed.

Or will you?

Self-hypnosis can stop the anxiety cycle and restore your equilibrium. It can reinforce the Touch-Control Method when the desire for food is especially strong. Here's how it works.

When you're in a state of goal conflict, you feel torn between two equally desirable goals. But are the goals really equal? Is your desire for one really as strong as your desire for the other? Self-hypnosis gives you time and distance and lets you evaluate the situation. Losing weight is the important long-term goal, while soothing yourself with food is just a whim. The goals are not equal at all. In fact, one of them is not even a real goal; it is an immediate urge seeking immediate gratification. Now that you realize this, it becomes easier to make the right decision. You are now able to let go of the idea of eating a jelly doughnut.

Why did you want to eat the doughnut in the first place? Because you wanted to escape from your harried world through food. Self-hypnosis will let you achieve that same escape but you will not have to use food to do it. You can use self-hypnosis to ease stress, to renew and refresh yourself, and to restore your sense of mastery and control. In this way, practicing self-hypnosis makes you a double winner.

How to Put Yourself in a Hypnotic State

Keeping in mind that you will be in control at all times and that nothing frightening or unpleasant will happen, are you willing to try the simple focusing and relaxation technique known as self-hypnosis?

(Your answer) _____

Before you perform the steps described below, I want you to know exactly what to expect. Please take time right now to read the remainder of this chapter and familiarize yourself with the process of going into and coming out of a self-hypnotic state. Walk through the steps several times in your mind. It's very important that you understand completely how to enter the state and how to leave it.

There are eight basic steps to putting yourself in a self-hypnotic state. Let's go through them one by one.

• *Step 1.* Get in the right position. This can be either sitting in a chair or lying on a bed or couch. Choose whichever position feels most comfortable to you. If you are sitting, look directly in front of you. Your neck and head should be straight but not stiff. If you are lying down, lie on your back, looking straight up at the ceiling.

- *Step 2.* Whether you are sitting or lying down, continue to look straight ahead. Now let your eyes roll up and back. Pretend you are trying to look up over your eyebrows—right over the top of your head. Do not strain your eyes. Just look up and back as far as feels comfortable to you.

- *Step 3.* Without feeling any strain or discomfort, continue looking up and over your eyebrows. As you do this, let your eyelids drop gently and slowly down, like two soft and restful curtains. Let them drop farther and farther, until they are completely down. Even though your lids are closed, your eyes are still looking comfortably up.

- *Step 4.* Now, with your eyelids still closed, take a deep breath through your nose. Do not open your mouth; simply inhale deeply and peacefully through your nose, the way a sleeping child might. Do not fill your lungs too full or strain yourself in any way. When you have inhaled, hold your breath a few seconds. Again, don't push yourself beyond the limits of your own comfort level. This is not a contest and there is no pressure on you at all.

- *Step 5.* Begin to exhale, letting the air escape easily through slightly parted lips. Continue exhaling while, with your eyelids still closed, you let your eyes roll down to their usual straight-ahead position.

- *Step 6.* While your eyelids are still closed and you are breathing at your normal, relaxed rate, imagine your body sinking deeper and deeper into your chair or couch. Enjoy the feelings of peace and tranquility that come to you. Not only your body but your mind as well is totally at ease. You feel free and unburdened, almost as if you are buoyantly floating. Yet you are also aware of being alert and completely focused.

- *Step 7.* The floating feeling is restful and pleasant. As you continue to enjoy it, shift your attention to either your left or right arm, whichever seems more natural to you. Imagine that your arm, from your fingertips to your elbow, is becoming lighter and lighter. It is completely weightless. Let it float up into the air by bending your elbow.

- *Step 8.* Your elbow is resting comfortably on your bed or couch, and your arm, fingers relaxed and wrist limp, is floating effortlessly in the air. It will remain there throughout the hypnotic state, just as your eyelids will remain closed. You have reached your chosen destination. You are in the pleasant, relaxed, and healing state known as self-hypnosis. You are free to focus your powerful, positive mental energy on the goal you have chosen for yourself.

How long did it take you to read through these eight steps? Two minutes? Three? Four? As you read, the steps may have seemed complex and time consuming. That's only because the process is new to you. Once you are familiar with it, it is really very simple. The eight separate steps flow together and do not take long to perform at all—only about thirty seconds. Of course, as with anything else you are learning, it will take a little longer at first. That's normal. Pretty soon, you'll be an experienced veteran!

While You Are in the Hypnotic State

Being in a hypnotic state offers you a unique opportunity to communicate with your inner self, to reaffirm your goals and build your motivation. You may wish to script several "programs" for yourself, each centering around the key words and themes that are important to you. Until you gain experience, however, I recommend that you use the program described below.

After you complete the eight steps and are in a hypnotic state, focus on the three Stoplines of the Touch-Control Method.

For my body, overeating is an insult and a poison.

I need my body to live.

I owe my body this respect and attention.

Pause for a moment.

Continue with this thought:

> To reach my goal of _____ pounds, I have to learn to be a thin eater. I am fully aware of the difference between thin eating and the overeating that is a poison to me. From now on, I want to practice only thin, healthful eating. In this way, I will reach my goal.

Now turn your attention one more time to the three crucial Stoplines:

> For my body, overeating is an insult and a poison.
>
> I need my body to live.
>
> I owe my body this respect and attention.

Realize that you have within you the motivation to reach your goal. Pause for a few moments to acknowledge this and reflect upon what it means to you. You are now ready to come out of the hypnotic state.

You can follow this brief, simple program just by focusing on it and repeating the words to yourself, or you can make a tape of your own voice, reading the appropriate words and thoughts and pausing in the proper places. Many people find this method to be a helpful tool indeed.

Returning from the Hypnotic State

Coming back always seems easier than going somewhere, and self-hypnosis is no exception. There are only seven steps to returning from the hypnotic state and they are simple to perform. They are labeled Step R1, Step R2, and so on to avoid any possible confusion.

- *Step R1.* With your arm still in the upright, floating position and your eyelids closed, take a deep breath through your nose. Remember not to strain or overexert yourself as you do this. Now, as before, hold your breath for a moment, just as long as is comfortable to you.
- *Step R2.* As you are performing the breathing exercise in Step R1 above, roll your eyes up and back beneath your closed eyelids. Imagine your eyes looking up over your eyebrows and back over the top of your head. Don't strain your eyes; there's no pressure here. Just roll your eyes up as far as your personal comfort zone allows.
- *Step R3.* Now let your breath escape through your parted lips. Don't force the air out, just let your breath flow naturally from between slightly parted lips. As you do this, slowly, s-l-o-w-l-y open your eyelids.
- *Step R4.* Feeling relaxed and refreshed and totally at ease, bring your eyes back down into the straight-ahead position and allow your vision to come back into focus.
- *Step R5.* Gently begin opening and closing the hand that is in the floating position. Do not tense or clench any of your muscles. Just flex a few times gently and pleasurably.
- *Step R6.* Without any force or pressure, let your floating arm return to a resting position on the surface of your chair or couch.
- *Step R7.* Remain sitting or lying for a few minutes as you enjoy this very pleasurable feeling. You deserve these few moments of restful repose before rushing back to your daily chores.

Like putting yourself into the hypnotic state, returning from the state is a swift and simple procedure. The whole process (entering, focusing on your goals, and returning) can be performed in a few minutes—which is why so many people have found self-hypnosis such a useful tool in combating stress, anxiety, and other resistance blocks that threaten to keep them from their goals.

Enjoy!

Once people understand self-hypnosis and become familiar with it, most find it not only helpful but pleasurable and enjoyable. And, of course, they are eager to practice their newly learned technique.

"How often can I do this?" is a question people often ask. "Will I wear out the 'magic' if I do it too often?" No, just the opposite. The more often one practices self-hypnosis, the stronger the magic becomes (although, of course, it really isn't magic at all). This is because you become more experienced at entering and returning from the state, and more skilled at focusing on the positive messages you give yourself while in it. Each time you enter the hypnotic state and establish contact with your inner self, you are reaffirming your goals in a uniquely effective way and renewing the source of your motivation.

Have a good time with what you have just learned today. Practice self-hypnosis several times and enjoy the experience totally. To help you, I've included a quick guide to entering and returning from the hypnotic state. This guide does not attempt to explain each step in detail, but is merely meant to act as a reminder. Feel free to clip this page out of the book and keep it near you as you practice self-hypnosis.

QUICK GUIDE FOR ENTERING A HYPNOTIC STATE

- *Step 1.* Assume a comfortable position sitting or lying down on your back.
- *Step 2.* Roll your eyes up and back.
- *Step 3.* Let your eyelids drop s-l-o-w-l-y, keeping your eyes looking up all the while.
- *Step 4.* Inhale deeply through your nose and hold the breath for a few moments.
- *Step 5.* Exhale slowly through slightly parted lips. As you do, let your eyes roll back down under your closed lids.
- *Step 6.* Imagine your body sinking down comfortably in your couch or chair.
- *Step 7.* Focus your mind on your hand and let your hand and arm become light and float up.
- *Step 8.* With eyelids still closed and arm in the floating position, you are now in the restful hypnotic state.

QUICK GUIDE FOR RETURNING FROM A HYPNOTIC STATE

- *Step R1.* With your eyelids closed and your arm floating comfortably, you decide to emerge from the trance.
- *Step R2.* Inhale deeply through your nose and hold the breath for a moment or two (as you did in step 4 to enter the trance).
- *Step R3.* Exhale slowly through slightly parted lips (as you did in step 5 to enter the trance).
- *Step R4.* Let your eyes roll up slowly, looking straight ahead as you open your eyelids.
- *Step R5.* Make a loose fist with your raised hand. Open the fist and let your fingers and hand relax. Now let your arm settle back gently into the starting position . . . and arise when you wish . . . to go about your day as usual. You are now out of the hypnotic state, alert and thoroughly refreshed.

DAY
SIX

VISUALIZATION DAY

Today's the day to:
- Fill in Day 6 of your 7-Day Food Diary.
- Make a goal list.
- Learn how visualization can work for you.

I'M PROUD of you. When people begin a new undertaking, the dropout rate is always heaviest at the beginning. Undoubtedly, a few well-intentioned people who bought this book have not made it this far. But you have. As soon as you began reading today, you passed the halfway mark. Your commitment is strong—strong enough to carry you through the rest of the 10-day diet countdown and forward into your program. So use the space below to write yourself a brief note of congratulations. Don't be stingy with the praise—you deserve it!

A Note of Congratulations to Myself

_____

_____

_____

Now go on with this chapter. Don't forget to fill in Day 6 of your 7-Day Food Diary, which you'll find on the next page.

7-DAY FOOD DIARY

For each entry, include the food you ate as well as all beverages, the time and circumstances, and any important feelings you had.

DAY 6

Day _____ Date _____

Breakfast _____

_____

Between _____

_____

Lunch _____

_____

Between _____

_____

Dinner _____

_____

Between _____

_____

Thoughts _____

_____

_____

GREAT EXPECTATIONS

Take a few minutes to complete the sentences below. Do not think out your answers beforehand. Instead, write down the first response that comes into your mind.

1. My body is _____

_____

2. To me, food means _____

_____

3. The first thing people think when they meet me is _____

_____

4. For me, dieting is _____

_____

5. If I had to compare my willpower to something, it would be a _____

6. If I woke up slim tomorrow I would _____

_____

7. I am a _____ eater.

After you have finished, look back at your answers with a critical eye. Become your own therapist for the next few minutes. What do your spontaneous answers reveal about the way you think and feel about yourself?

What word, for example, did you use to complete the very last question? Was it something like *binge*, *hopeless*, or *fat*?

How about the second question? What does food mean to you? Does it mean *everything*? Does it mean *temptation* or *torture*, *fun* or *fat*?

In question 4, did you write that dieting means *deprivation* or *temptation*? And if you woke up thin tomorrow, what would you do? If you said *eat*, you're not alone. Many people have this very same reaction.

Some of your answers may be irrefutably perceptive. But I'm willing to bet that at least a few of your answers are exaggerations. Is the person who sees himself as a *blimp* really equal in size to the Hindenburg? Is the person who describes herself as a *hopeless* eater always hopeless?

Your answers to these questions reveal more than facts. They reveal the expectations you have about yourself: how you expect to look, how you expect to be perceived by others, how you expect to react to food, and how you expect to feel while you are dieting.

Again, acting as your own objective therapist, examine your answers and write down, in the space below, what kind of expectations you have about your body, food, dieting, and the opinions of others.

Notes

_____

_____

_____

_____

_____

_____

_____

_____

_____

You are probably familiar with the phrase "self-fulfilling prophecy." And you have probably seen it in action more than a few times. Many overweight people are victims of their own self-fulfilling prophecies. They expect to be overweight. They expect their clothes to be either baggy or eternally too tight. They expect food to overwhelm them with temptation. And when they diet, no matter how much they would *like* to succeed, they expect to fail.

Over the next three days, you're going to learn how to break free from this cycle. You are not only going to get rid of your negative expectations, you are going to replace them with positive ones. You are going to turn what is now a destructive force into a positive source of motivation.

Visualization and How It Works

Visualization is really just another word for self-fulfilling prophecy. When you visualize something, you place it your mind and devote a certain amount of mental energy—either conscious or subconscious—to it.

Let's take a minute to see how the process works. A waitress carrying a heavy tray down a flight of stairs is warned by a well-meaning co-worker not to trip. Her chances of tripping are immediately increased. Why? Because the waitress, who hadn't been thinking of tripping at all, is now focused on the possibility. She imagines her ankle turning, her tray unbalancing, and plates and dishes crashing to the bottom of the stairs. She *visualizes* herself falling, so she will now have to exercise great caution not to fulfill that visualization.

The outcome of visualization can be either positive or negative, but the process is the same. The mind runs forward to embrace an image, an event, or a feeling. Even though this image, event, or feeling does not exist in reality, the mind treats it as if it does. The mind gives it meaning, form, texture, and respect. Led by the mind's powerful imagining, the body compliantly follows.

Many people have found a way to direct this powerful force. While watching the last winter Olympics on television, I noticed how often athletes used the power of positive visualization. Perhaps you noticed, too, how the slalom skiers and lugers would stand a few moments before the race with their eyes closed, envisioning the course before them and how their bodies would respond to each challenge. These people were using the tool of visualization. Not only did they see the course ahead but they saw their bodies moving swiftly, effortlessly, and powerfully past each obstacle.

You will probably never be an Olympic athlete. Your goal is much different. But it is just as challenging and every bit as important. Are you ready to use the tool of visualization to achieve your goal?

(Your answer) _____

If you answered no, stop here and spend some time thinking about visualization. Can you remember a time in your life when you used visualization in a positive way—daydreaming about your wedding day or about a wonderful vacation, for example? Can you see how visualization prepared and readied you for the upcoming event? Can you remember what a pleasurable experience it was to imagine having your goal at hand?

When you are ready to use visualization, go on to the next section.

Your Personal Prize Package

Before you can put visualization to work, you must know what your goal is. Let's start with the main one.

I now weigh _____ pounds and my desire is to weigh _____ pounds. I am going to lose _____ pounds.

Today's date: _____

Signature: _____

That's good, but it's a big goal, isn't it? It will be a while before you have the satisfaction of seeing it accomplished.

Look at the goal again. Imagine it as a large, beautifully wrapped gift. Imagine the paper and the ribbon in your favorite colors. Perhaps there is a fresh flower worked into the arrangement, or a stunning ornament. Now look at the name tag.

To _____

Make sure you write your name on the tag! After all, this present is for you.

Now begin unwrapping this big, big box. When you open it, you see that it contains many other boxes, each wrapped just as splendidly as the larger box. These smaller boxes are goals, too. They are the many and varied desires that led you to the decision to lose weight. (Remember: A goal is just a gift you want to give yourself.)

Let's open these smaller boxes and see exactly what's inside each one. The contents will be just a little different for each person who is reading this book. One might find a box that has this goal inside: "To fit into my blue skirt again." Someone else might find the desire to "walk a mile without feeling tired." Still another might wish for "a wolf whistle from my favorite person."

I want you to use the spaces on page 113 to write down the goals you find inside your personal set of packages. Here are some areas of your life you might think of as you do this exercise:

- Your looks
- Physical health
- Energy
- Sexuality
- How your clothes look, fit, and feel
- Eating behavior
- Relationships with friends and family

- Love relationships
- On-the-job relationships
- Your career
- Self-confidence

Notice that there is plenty of room to write down your goals. You don't have to fill in all the blanks at once. Whenever one of your goals comes to mind, jot it down. If you run out of room—and I really hope you do—continue your list on another sheet of paper or in a blank book. Each time you identify a goal, you strengthen your motivation to achieve your overall goal of losing weight.

There are just a few rules for writing down the goals you find in your Personal Prize Package. They aren't difficult, but they *are* important.

- *Work in miniature.* Don't try to paint the whole picture at once. Instead of writing "to be thin," focus on the first step toward that large goal, such as "to lose my first five pounds." After you lose those five pounds, mark that particular goal "achieved" and create a new goal: "to lose my first ten pounds."
- *Make sure you really want it.* Don't write down goals that you don't really want. Seeing a list of false goals will undermine your motivation rather than strengthen it.
- *Be specific.* Avoid vagueness at all costs! Instead of stating that you want to buy new clothes, focus on a particular garment you would like to shop for. What size is it? What does it look like? Add enough details to make this goal real to you.
- *Be positive.* Don't use negative words or images. For example, instead of writing that you "don't want to feel like a fat pig anymore," write that you *do* "want to feel slim."
- *Date each entry.*
- *Keep it private.* This is for your eyes and your eyes only.

• *Don't limit yourself.* If it's something you really want, no goal is too large—or too trivial—for you to acknowledge.

Now that you know the rules, have a good time writing down all the things in your Personal Prize Package.

PERSONAL PRIZE PACKAGE GOAL LIST

Date	Goal	Date Achieved

Maintaining Your Goal List

Be sure to maintain your goal list as you begin your weight-loss program. Look back at your goals often. Whenever you have achieved one of them, put a star by it and record the date. Always be sure to add new goals to your list. If you discover that you no longer want a particular goal, draw a line through it. Above all, have a good time with your list—it's the Personal Prize Package that will keep your motivation going strong!

How to Use Visualization

Now that you have identified what some of your goals are, you can use the power of visualization to help them become reality.

How? The technique is really very simple and enjoyable. Pick one of the goals from the list you just worked on. After you have selected one, use your imagination to picture that goal clearly and vividly. Using an example such as "lose five pounds" (but it can be any goal that is important to you), you might imagine exactly what you would see if you were to step on a scale and weigh five pounds less than you do today. Can you picture your toes? Can you picture the numbers on the scale and the needle pointing to a particular number?

Now go on to broaden your mental image. Imagine your face looking just a little slimmer and your clothes being just a little looser and more comfortable. Now imagine how you will *feel* when you achieve that goal: sensations of pride, success, and self-esteem. End the visualization on a positive note. Say, "This goal is within my grasp. I have only to continue the course I have begun to achieve it."

Focus on the goal you have chosen several times a day. Always create a clear mental image of it and give that image as many details as you can. Imagine how things will be, how you will act, and how you will feel. Always end by reminding yourself that the goal is within your grasp.

Perhaps the goal involves changing your basic self-image—say, from a couch potato to someone who is much more active. Use the same imaging technique to see yourself leading a more active lifestyle: going up stairs, walking briskly, getting up to change channels instead of relying on the remote control. Always be sure to put your emotions into the visualization. Don't just see yourself doing these things—see yourself doing them and enjoying them!

You can also use visualization to overcome potential obstacles. Just as an athlete anticipates the hurdles in a race and imagines his body sailing over them, so you can use this special kind of rehearsal to resist temptation when it comes your way.

Recently, a patient of mine named Jack used visualization to get through an upcoming banquet. Jack knew exactly what the banquet would be like. "There'll be loads of good, rich food and an open bar. Everyone from my boss to my wife will be urging me to eat, drink, and be merry—and I'm afraid that's just what I'll do."

Jack practiced visualizing a "perfect script" for his behavior. He pictured himself eating only the types and amounts of food consistent with his diet. He saw himself circulating and having a good time but turning down extra food and liquor. He created a scenario in which his wife pressed him to take a second helping, then he rehearsed the words he would use to decline her offer gently but firmly.

In the days before the banquet, Jack focused on this visualization often. He almost forget to put his feelings of pride and success into the picture, but did so when reminded to. By the time the banquet arrived, Jack found himself well rehearsed and able to resist the temptation to overeat. He told me it was the first such event he had ever come away from without a "food hangover."

Still another way to use visualization is to give form and substance to an intangible idea. Let's use the concept of motivation as an example. Many people have a hard time with motivation because it can't been seen, touched, felt, or measured in any finite way—you can hardly go to a bank and ask to see how much motivation you have on hand! Because motivation is intangible, it is especially hard to comprehend. Yet, if your motivation is going to work for you, you need to believe in it thoroughly.

Another of my patients, Sylvia, discovered an ingenious solution to the dilemma. She arrived in my office one day with a picture she had painted. The picture showed a beautiful fountain with plumes of water shooting high into the air. It was clearly a powerful fountain, as evidenced by the height of its jets. Yet it was also graceful and very feminine. "What a lovely picture," I said. "Does this fountain exist? I would love to visit it."

Sylvia laughed and said that, although the fountain did exist, a visit was quite impossible. "This fountain is my motivation," she explained. "Since it's really a part of me, I decided to give it a shape. I began with small brush strokes—very modest jets of water, you see. But this is what I ended up with. Until I painted this picture I had no idea how beautiful or powerful my motivation is."

Different Ways to Visualize

There is no one single way to visualize. For Sylvia, seeing was believing. For Jack, the common practice of mental imaging worked. Today, choose one of the ways to visualize listed below, and use it to focus on one of your goals.

- *Mental imaging.* Like Jack, pick a goal or situation and focus your imagination on it. Be sure to follow the basic steps described on pages 114–115 of this chapter.
- *Seeing.* Perhaps you think only a gifted artist can paint or sketch his vision. That's not true. Sylvia wasn't an artist at all, yet she created a wonderful picture of her motivation. This is your chance to explore your artistic side: abstract, psychedelic, impressionistic, or primitive. Buy yourself some colored pencils or magic markers and have a good time. If this idea is totally unappealing to you, cut and paste your ideal vision from magazine pictures and photographs. If your goal is to lose forty pounds and tour the Caribbean in a

red string bikini, find pictures of a beach and a bikini-clad model and finish
the scene by pasting a picture of your face onto the body.

- *Writing.* For many people, writing is an especially vivid way to visualize. Begin by writing your chosen goal at the top of the page, then let your
pen describe the details. Be lavish—use vivid words and don't hesitate to include feelings, characters, and a dialogue!

- *Hearing.* Make a tape for yourself to listen to. On this tape, describe
the goal you have chosen in lush detail. Try several ways of addressing yourself.
For example, you might say, "I have lost ten pounds and feel very attractive
and sexy." Later, you might talk to yourself as one person addressing another,
saying, "Lois, I can see you've lost ten pounds! You look very attractive and
sexy." And later, you might speak as someone addressing a third party. "Have
you seen Lois? She's lost ten pounds. You can tell just by looking at her that
she feels very attractive. Everyone says she looks great, and the men can't stop
talking about how sexy she is!"

- *Combining.* Use mental imaging *plus* a sensory cue like taste, sound,
etc. For example, prepare a food that is healthy but not particularly appealing
to you—one of the foods, perhaps, that you will be eating on your diet. As you
taste it, conjure up an image of your goal. With each bite, imagine yourself
having and enjoying that goal. (This kind of exercise will help you shift the
focus away from "forbidden" foods by linking your goal with the foods that
will help you achieve it.) Another way would be to set the scene for this
visualization with soothing background music.

Whatever method you choose, have a good time with it. Don't let feelings
of doubt or low self-esteem spoil your enjoyment. Often people get caught up
in feelings such as, "I don't deserve it." You *do* deserve to feel good about
yourself. You have done a lot of important work over the past six days and
armed yourself with the tools of success. I have acted as your teacher and your
guide, but the rest was strictly your own hard work. Just continue and you will
achieve each of the goals you visualize.

DAY
SEVEN

GET IN TOUCH WITH YOUR BODY DAY

Today's the day to:

- Complete your 7-Day Food Diary.
- Use visualization for your new body image.
- Blast food cravings with Supportlines.
- Get in touch with your body through exercise.

YOU HAVE arrived at the last day of your 7-Day Food Diary. Tomorrow, we'll analyze the information you've gathered. Today, I want you to take a moment to acknowledge what you've done.

When you began this program, the idea of keeping a food diary was probably anything but appealing. You wanted a quick diagnosis that would yield instant results. But you agreed to cooperate. No doubt there were days when keeping the diary was a real struggle for you. In spite of this, you persevered. Now you have only today's diary to complete and you'll have a week's worth of important information about when, why, and how you eat.

Are you ready to finish your 7-Day Food Diary?

(Your answer) _____

Good. Turn the page.

7-DAY FOOD DIARY

For each entry, include the food you ate as well as all beverages, the time and circumstances, and any important feelings you had.

DAY 7

Day _____ Date _____

Breakfast _____

_____

Between _____

_____

Lunch _____

_____

Between _____

_____

Dinner _____

_____

Between _____

_____

Thoughts _____

_____

_____

GETTING TO KNOW YOU

How well do you know your body? Take a moment to complete this brief questionnaire. Do not do any "research"—just write down the answers you feel are correct.

1. I am _____ pounds overweight.

2. My goal weight is _____ pounds. The last time I was at this weight was _____ .

2. My measurements are:

_____ bust   _____ waist   _____ hips
_____ thigh   _____ upper arm

3. The parts of my body that I like are my:

_____   _____   _____

_____   _____   _____

_____   _____   _____

4. The parts of my body I am going to improve are my:

_____   _____   _____

_____   _____   _____

_____   _____   _____

5. The last time I looked at myself nude in a full-length mirror was:

_____

6. It is (easy–difficult–impossible) for me to see myself as I will look when I have achieved my goal weight.

How did you do on the questions? Many people discover they don't know nearly as much about their bodies as they thought! Do you fall into this category?

It's ironic but true that many overweight people—the very people who feel trapped and victimized by their physical being—have a faculty perception of their bodies. They don't know what their true measurements are, and they have a mistaken perception of how they look in their clothes.

If you discovered you don't know yourself as well as you thought, don't feel bad. By the end of today, you will have clearer answers to all of the queries on the questionnaire.

To get acquainted with your body you will need some simple equipment: a tape measure, a scale, a full-length mirror, a hand mirror, and room in which you can be alone and undisturbed.

Begin by weighing yourself and calculating the difference between your present weight and your goal weight. How many pounds do you have to lose?

The purpose of this is to make sure your chosen goal weight is realistic for your body. Not all people have an accurate idea of how much weight they should lose and this creates problems. For example, many people, particularly women, set extreme goals for themselves. Not everybody is meant to look like a seventeen-year-old fashion model, and trying to battle your body below it's own healthy weight range will only leave you feeling like a failure.

The charts in Appendix II should help you determine a healthy weight for your sex, height, and frame. But keep in mind that these tables only reflect the averages of millions of people. Your personal ideal body weight might be slightly higher or slightly lower. My definition of ideal weight is: the weight that *you* feel most comfortable at and that you can maintain.

Now, how about your measurements? Again, many people don't have an accurate idea of their proportions. It's not a simple case of denial, either. Ironically, many people think they are larger than they actually are. They see their bodies as vast and ever-expanding, and this mind-set becomes a self-fulfilling prophecy. Were your guesses about your measurements accurate? Were they too large or too small?

Now, I want you to observe yourself nude in a full-length mirror.

Was that a howl of protest I heard? The usual response I get is, "Well, I have avoided this for a long time. I only look in the mirror when I absolutely have to and then only from the neck up."

Is that how you feel too? What do you think the motive could be for asking you to do this?

The motive is: _____

_____

The correct answer is that you need to become *aware* of your body and be in touch with its physical shape.

Let's talk about it.

First of all, I don't want to make you ashamed of yourself or your body. Just the opposite. I want you to get in touch with your body and learn to love, respect, and protect it.

Perhaps you believe you are *too much* in touch with your body already. People who want to lose weight often have complex, quite specific ideas on this score. One person feels angry at his body for gaining weight. Another feels her body is beyond her control. Still another feels she has betrayed her body by cramming it with unnecessary food and forcing its organs to work overtime. The common thread among these attitudes is the sharp line dividing the mind and the body.

Mary Pat, a talented artist in her mid thirties, revealed during a group session that her apartment was devoid of full-length mirrors. The mirrors she did allow were all hung at eye level. "Why?" asked Lila, another member of the group. "Because I stop at my neck," Mary Pat answered simply.

This patient expressed, in a few words, the estrangement that often takes place between the body and the mind. Mary Pat, creator of beautiful artwork, refused to acknowledge the body she saw reflected in the mirror. Long ago she had divorced herself from her body. She no longer listened to its demands, she no longer acknowledged its needs, she no longer took responsibility for its care. The disastrous result of all this led her to my group session.

The truth is that you cannot dissociate yourself from your body. If you've lost touch, now's the time to begin a reconciliation. Unless you have concern, respect, and love for your body, how can you properly take care of it?

There's another reason why you need to be in touch with your body, and that's to prepare for the changes that lie ahead. Perhaps you think you need no preparation. "If I could look in the mirror and see a thin me," a patient named Rick said, "I'd be the happiest person on earth."

Unfortunately, this isn't what happened. Rick was unprepared for his new body, and the closer and closer he came to his goal weight, the more distressed and apprehensive he became. The reason was that, once thin, he had to confront some of his underlying conflicts about dating and intimacy. Since he wasn't ready to face these conflicts, he broke his diet and ate his way back up the scale.

When you diet, you are changing the shape and nature of the physical "house" you live in. Unless you prepare yourself as you go along, unless you get ready to accept this new house, it will not seem right to you. Like Rick, you may be subconsciously resistant to it. Or you may be unprepared for your new image and end up feeling like a stranger in your own body. Or you may be so used to the "fat" mental image you have of yourself, you will not even see the progress you have made! It is not at all uncommon for a person who has lost a great deal of weight to continue to see his or her old self in the mirror. All of these discomforting experiences can lead you right back up the scale.

The one and only purpose of the exercises you are doing today is to help you visualize your body in a positive and loving way. As you learned yesterday, the process of visualization is powerful. It can keep your motivation strong and help you achieve seemingly impossible goals.

Now, are you ready to go on?

(Your answer) _____

Good. I want you to take off your clothes and observe your body in a full-length mirror. Use the hand mirror to see how you look in profile and from the back.

There is one thing you must not do during this exercise, and that is be overly harsh or critical. Notice that I used the words *observe your body*—not *criticize its flaws*.

Remember:
What I see in the mirror is *my* body. No matter what shape it is in, it is serving me well. It carries me through each day. It pumps blood to my brain and allows beautiful thoughts to form. Its muscles follow my commands to the best of their ability. It gives me the physical pleasures of sight, sound, scent, taste, and touch. If my body is not in the shape I would like it to be in, it is not my body's fault. I am the caretaker of my body. If my care has been imperfect, I am now ready to give my body the attention and respect it deserves.

As you think of this and observe your body, reinforce your motivation to diet by repeating the Stoplines:

For my body, overeating is an insult and a poison.

I need my body to live.

I owe my body this respect and attention.

Use the space below to decide which areas of your body you like and which you are going to improve. Observe each part of your body, beginning with the top of your head and moving slowly downward. For each area you wish to improve, try to find an area you are happy with. If you feel your thighs are too heavy, for example, remind yourself that their heaviness does not cancel out your exotic eyes or your smooth skin.

Here are some other "lovely points" that people frequently overlook: well-kept nails, sensuous hair, white teeth, great smile, good posture, elegant neck, shapely ankles, creamy shoulders. Notice that I have attached a positive adjective (great, good, sensuous, etc.) to each point. Please follow my example and do the same when describing your own lovely points!

Lovely Points	Points to Improve

Don't be afraid to touch your body, particularly the parts you wish to change. If you want a flatter stomach, lay your hands on your stomach as you consider this. Feel the warm, loving energy flowing through your palms. Close your eyes briefly. Imagine your stomach growing flatter and firmer as you help it with diet and exercise. Imagine how you will look as you move closer and closer to this goal.

If this exercise makes you uncomfortable, you aren't alone. Many people find this a difficult step to take, either because they have been out of touch with their bodies for so long or because they are hampered by feelings of shame, guilt, or anger.

Even if they don't make it the first time they try this exercise, I encourage them to try again, just as I am going to encourage you.

I once had a patient named Abby, who at 5′6″ weighed around 195. She had always been heavy and had a very poor concept of her body as a physical entity. When she had trouble with the exercise with the full-length mirror, I encouraged her to go for a body massage. She decided to do so and afterwards reported that it had been an eye-opening experience. For the first time in her life, Abby felt in touch with the external boundaries of her body. This new perspective made it possible for her to lose weight, adjust to, and accept her new body shape.

I encourage you to do this exercise for exactly the same reasons. Understanding the external boundaries of your body will help you to see that body clearly, and this in turn will help you to respect and protect it.

Don't be surprised if approaching your body with loving concern instead of shame and loathing fills you with emotion. This is a healing step, a truce that marks the end of a long and bitter civil war. Remind yourself that this is the beginning of a new era—an era of peace and communication between your mind and your body, an era of love and positive achievement.

As you diet, come back to your mirror often. Continue to observe yourself in this special way, taking pride in your body as it changes and accepting each part of it with love.

I cannot emphasize strongly enough how important it is for you to prepare yourself for your "new" body as well. Unless you learn to see it as *yours*, you will be uncomfortable with it. As you diet, do at least one visualization a day in which you imagine and welcome the healthier, slimmer body you are working so hard to achieve.

The mirror exercise described above is one way, but there is a simpler technique, one you can do anywhere. I call it *televisualization*. Sit in a comfortable chair, close your eyes, and practice the relaxation breathing you learned on Day 5 (pages 97–101). Let the worries and tensions of the day slide away and summon up the image of a large, blank screen. See yourself on that screen as you look at your current weight without clothes. View yourself, as always, with objectivity but also with love. Now see yourself slimming down, pound by pound, until you've reached your desired shape.

Can you visualize the changes that will take place? Your profile losing its double chin? Your waist narrowing? Very good. Remember to see the *whole* process—no startling "before" and "after" pictures here, please!

If it is difficult for you to visualize yourself at your ideal body weight, do it gradually. Initially, try to imagine how your body will look once you have lost the first five, ten, or twenty pounds. You can also look at an old picture of yourself, taken when you were a bit slimmer, or you can go to a clothing store and hold up dresses one or two sizes smaller than what you wear now. This will give you an idea of your future body shape.

What Your Clothes Say About You

Write a brief description of the clothes you are wearing right now.

_____

_____

_____

Are these clothes typical of your usual manner of dressing?

_____

List the three or four outfits you wear most often.

_____

_____

_____

How a person dresses reveals a lot. First of all, it reveals what's available in the clothing stores. If you are very overweight and cannot wear standard sizes, you may have had a hard time dressing attractively. I understand that.

Even so, some people come into my office looking unnecessarily bedraggled. Missing buttons, drab colors, and lack of makeup and accessories all proclaim: "I've stopped trying! I don't deserve to look good!"

Some people try to hide a body they think is shapeless and unattractive beneath loose, oversize clothing. On the other side of the coin is the person whose clothes are chronically too tight. This person may have true denial about his size or he may feel that buying snug clothes will somehow force him to diet. It's a nice theory, but it doesn't work. When you wear clothes that are too tight, you feel miserable, fat, and unattractive, and the frustration of feeling uncomfortable in your clothes may push you to eat, not diet.

Think of your style of dressing. Do you take care to make yourself look and feel as attractive as possible? Do you wear belts or shun them? Does your wardrobe include a variety of styles or do you limit yourself to a few safe options? What is your color range? Do you wear bright colors or do you stay with camouflage shades of black, gray, and navy blue?

Only you know your body and what truly enhances it. Take a moment to evaluate your style of dressing and decide what it says about your attitude towards your body.

What My Clothes Say About Me

    I'm not advocating that anyone wear clothes she feels uncomfortable in, but clothes that conceal your shape can work against you. They discourage body pride and give you permission to grow bigger. They allow you to detach yourself from your body. They even allow you to gain weight without being aware of it. A pair of pants with an elastic waistband, for example, will accommodate a startling number of unwanted pounds!

Just as it would help you to stop *thinking* of yourself as a fat eater and begin seeing yourself as a thin eater, it would help to stop *dressing* like a fat person and begin dressing as an attractive person who deserves to look his or her best at any weight. Taking care with your dressing (even if you are limited in the immediate changes you can make in your wardrobe) is yet another way of beginning to improve that all-important self-image of yours.

All right, let's take a look in your closet. If you're like many dieters, you have a wide range of clothing sizes from which to choose. Clothes that fit you once. Clothes you hope will fit you again. "Emergency clothes" that will fit you at any weight.

My feeling is that these emergency clothes are an invitation to gain weight, a subconscious plan for the inevitable. As you grow slimmer, I encourage you to get rid of them. Say a formal farewell to them and donate them to your favorite charity. After all, you won't need them again, will you?

Now let's look at the clothes that no longer fit you. Pick a dress, a pair of pants, or a suit that you particularly like. Hang it in a place where you can look at it or hold it in front of you as you observe yourself in the mirror. Visualize yourself growing slimmer and being able to wear and enjoy this garment once again. As you do this visualization, say to yourself:

> This dress (or suit or shirt) belongs to me. It was created for no one but me. It is mine and I will soon be able to wear it again.

Repossessing your clothes in this way can help keep your motivation going strong. Besides visualizing yourself nude, you will also want to visualize yourself wearing your favorite clothes. Imagine how you will look, the compliments you will receive, and the sensual feel of the fabric on your body.

You may also start adding attractive accessories to improve your appearance from the very start. One of my patients surprised me at each visit by wearing a new pair of smashing earrings. Regardless of your budget or wardrobe, be colorful and creative! Add a dramatic scarf to your navy office suit, buy bright new frames for your glasses, add a bangle at your wrist, clip a shimmering pin to your lapel. You'll be surprised to see what a difference a single added detail will make in the way you look and feel!

Is It Hunger or Is It Appetite?
Using Supportlines to Tell the Difference

So far, we've concentrated on the outside you. Now let's get in touch with the inside you—your body and its needs.

Your body's chief need is nourishment: liquid, sleep, and fuel. When your body needs liquid, it signals thirst; when it needs rest it signals sleepiness; and when your body needs fuel, it signals its hunger to you. Are you in touch with your body's need for fuel? Take a moment to complete the following sentence.

I am hungry:
      _____ almost always
      _____ frequently
      _____ sometimes
      _____ seldom
      _____ don't know

Many overweight people claim to be constantly hungry, but that is seldom actually true. Often, their craving stems from an emotional desire to eat, and this is called appetite. Or, there is an oral need that the person thinks is hunger but is in fact *thirst*. It is important to keep in mind that many overweight people misinterpret the need to drink as the need to eat. The body's water needs exceed the need for food, and you can survive much longer without food than you can without water. If you take care to drink more water (eight to ten glasses a day) you will eat less food!

Can you tell the difference between hunger and appetite? Many people cannot. They have confused hunger and appetite so often they can no longer tell when their bodies are truly in need of food.

Here are some of the things that can stimulate your *appetite:*

- Uncomfortable emotional states like loneliness, boredom, and sadness.
- Comfortable emotional states like happiness.
- Uncomfortable physical states like frustration, anxiety, and agitation.
- Comfortable physical states like being pleasurably warm or relaxed.
- The sight of food.
- The smell of food.
- The thought of food.
- Sounds related to food, such as the rustle of a candy wrapper or the sizzle of bacon.
- Habit.

Here is what stimulates true *hunger:*

- The body's depletion of its supply of nutrients and need for fuel.

It may help you to think of hunger as a process that begins in your stomach, and appetite as a process that begins in your mind.

It may also help to realize that when you are truly hungry you desire food that is generally healthy for you: fruit, protein, vegetables—all the things that make a well-balanced and satisfying meal. Also, when you are truly hungry you are likely to want food in general, rather than a specific food item.

When you experience appetite, on the other hand, your desire is likely to focus on a particular food item (a piece of chocolate cake, french fries, etc.) or on a group of foods that are *not* healthy for you (sweets, refined carbohydrates, fried foods, etc.). These foods are long on calories and short on nourishment and they invite overeating by teasing your appetite with the desire for more.

Can you now tell the difference between hunger and appetite?

(Your answer) _____

If you are going to be successful on your diet, you will have to learn to distinguish between appetite and hunger and cope with both sensations.

The good news is that hunger is not difficult to deal with. It is not nearly as gripping and torturous as appetite is. You can cope with your hunger by following a safe, nutritionally balanced diet and by putting up with the minor physical discomfort you will experience at first. (After the a few days of dieting, physical hunger usually diminishes.)

But how will you cope with your appetite? What will you do when you are seized by the desire to eat? At such times it's difficult to distinguish between hunger and appetite.

To help you remain in touch with your body, I have developed a special support-boost. Learn it right now and make it yours by practicing it several times today. In this way, the support-boost technique will come to you when you need it.

Begin by practicing the Touch-Control Method as you learned it on Day 3. Now continue in a relaxed state and follow these simple steps:

- *Step 1.* Briefly close your eyes and touch your finger to your face.
- *Step 2.* Visualize your body nude as it looks today. Focus in on your stomach and digestive area and ask yourself these three questions which I call Supportlines:

How hungry am I right now?

How much have I eaten so far today?

What am I going to eat the rest of the day?

- *Step 3.* Keep visualizing your body at its present weight.
- *Step 4.* Now, use the televisualization technique you learned on page 127 to see your body growing slimmer and slimmer. As you fully enjoy this visualization, tell yourself, "This is my positive goal. This is how I'm going to look and feel."
- *Step 5.* Remove your finger from your face, open your eyes, and feel the positive, supportive flow of renewed motivation.

Once you recognize that a food craving is triggered by appetite rather than hunger, you will be able to cope with it rationally. You will be able to see that a slimmer body is the goal you really want, not the momentary satisfaction of eating.

Getting in Touch Through Exercise

One of the best ways to get in touch with your body is through physical movement.

Many of my patients are resistant to exercise. Not only have they not built physical activity into their lives, they have devised ingenious ways of avoiding simple, everyday tasks. They are out of the habit of walking to the store, of climbing stairs, of doing their own housework and yardwork. One of my patients, intent on reaching her goal weight, was shocked by my suggestion that she stop paying someone to walk her dog and benefit from the exercise herself.

A typical objection to exercise was summed up by a young woman named Ellen. "It's a waste of time," she complained. "I could walk all day and not lose a pound." As proof she pointed to a chart that claimed a 120-pound woman would burn only about 150 calories during a brisk half-hour walk.

The chart was absolutely accurate but Ellen was absolutely wrong. If pursued on a regular basis, exercise promotes stabilization at a normal weight in a number of ways, which are listed below. Notice that there are a few blank lines. These are for you to write down the ways in which exercise will personally help you reach your goal. Don't think you have to sound like a medical expert when you fill them in. When I asked a friend of mine why he swam an hour every day he said, "If you're looking at the bottom of a pool, you can't eat, can you?"

- *Exercise promotes the burning of fat rather than muscle tissue.* The body has its own priorities. If muscles aren't being used, the body doesn't feed them. When you lose weight without exercising, you lose both fat and muscle tissue. When you increase your physical activity level, you maintain muscle tissue and burn more fat.
- *Building your muscle tissue is a benefit.* Muscles grow when challenged to perform. Trading a pound of fat for a pound of muscle will do more than firm you up—it will increase the number of calories you burn. Muscles utilize many more calories than fat tissue does, do improving your muscle tone means you will burn more fuel.
- *Increased movement boosts metabolism, the rate at which the body burns calories.* When the body burns calories at a slower rate, more calories end up being stored in fat tissue. Exercise helps accelerate the calorie-burning process. Studies show that this effect applies not only to the time during which you are active but carries over into your at-rest hours as well.
- *Activity helps control the appetite.* One of the great ironies of life is that inactivity, for many people, stimulates food cravings. It's no accident that watching television and snacking go hand in hand, just as it's no accident that movie theaters make fortunes from strategically placed concession stands. As you increase your level of physical activity you will experience a lessening of these cravings. Your will find it easier to say "no" to high-calorie, low-nutrient foods and "yes" to the foods your body really needs.
- *Exercise puts you in touch with your body.* As you increase your level of activity, you will become increasingly aware of your body—of its needs,

of the pleasure it can give, of the things it can accomplish. You will come to understand that you are in control of your body and the food that goes into it.

_____

_____

_____

_____

Now that you know the benefits exercise can bring, are you willing to put more physical activity into your life?

(Your answer) _____

When I say "put more physical activity into your life," that's exactly what I mean. I don't mean go out and jog two miles and I don't mean aerobicize yourself into a sore-muscled heap. Eventually, you should adopt a permanent program of healthful, well-balanced exercise, a program that will burn calories, limber up your muscles, and build your strength. But today, I am asking something far simpler—that you _use_ that marvelous, amazing body of yours more than you used it yesterday. Here's an idea of what I mean:

- Pace off the boundaries of your yard. Enjoy taking long, powerful strides.
- Write a postcard to a friend and walk to the corner mailbox.
- S-t-r-e-t-c-h.
- Dance.
- Instead of taking the elevator all the way to your office, walk one or two flights.
- Wash your car. Make a game of it and enjoy splashing around in the suds.
- Rent an exercise video.
- See how far you can walk in fifteen minutes.

- Buy a magazine with exercise tips in it and do the exercises.
- Go for a swim.

Whatever you decide to do, concentrate on the pleasurable aspects of it. As you walk (or swim or dance, whatever you choose), feel the energy flowing through you. Imagine your metabolism picking up, making efficient use of calories rather than storing them as fat. Visualize your organs working smoothly and in harmony, and your muscles growing firmer and sleeker. Be sure to reward yourself for your effort—take a relaxing shower or a soothing bath. This is not only good for your muscles; it will leave you feeling like a whole new person.

As the days go on and you begin your diet, you will find yourself feeling even more energetic because you are no longer weighed down with excess food. Don't be surprised if you find your former craving for food replaced with a craving for increased exercise. You wouldn't be the first person who's gotten hooked on the joy of physical movement!

Thank You Very Much

I began today by congratulating you for persevering through all seven days of your food diary. Now it's time for you to thank yourself.

Even though this assignment was neither convenient nor easy, *you did it!* You found time in your busy schedule, you overcame your own resistance, and you completed the task. You may not have completed it perfectly—you may have skipped an entry here or there, or forgotten to write something down. But each time you got off the track, you got back on again, and that's what's important.

In finishing your 7-Day Food Diary, you've done more than learn about your eating habits. You've learned how to achieve a goal by taking one step at a time and going on in spite of difficulties and lapses. In just this same way, you will be able to succeed with your diet when Take-Off Day arrives!

DAY EIGHT

POSITIVE SELF-IMAGE DAY

Today's the day to:

- Evaluate your 7-Day Food Diary.
- Eliminate negative self-talk.
- Change negative messages to positive ones.

Evaluate Your 7-Day Food Diary

YOU'VE FINISHED the hard work of keeping a food diary—now it's time to reap the benefits. The information the diary contains about your eating patterns will make it possible for you to identify and overcome your bad habits.

First, without looking at the diary itself, are there certain patterns you became aware of during the past week? What were they?

_____

_____

_____

If you were asked to identify the major cause of your overweight, what would it be? (See Day 1, pages 24–26.)

_____

_____

If you were asked to identify your destructive eating style, what would it be? (See Day 2, pages 46–48.)

_____

These questions are not being asked to make you feel bad or criticized. The answers are important only for the insight they provide—insight that, when combined with motivation, becomes a powerful tool for change.

Don't be surprised if you don't fit neatly into any single category. Overweight is often the result of a combination of factors: for example, a preference for carbohydrates _plus_ a predisposition to gain weight _plus_ a tendency to eat out of boredom. Seeing a number of traits or patterns in yourself doesn't mean you are doomed. It just means you need to be aware of each trouble spot so that you can mount a strategy against it.

Now, spend some time examining each day of your 7-Day Food Diary and complete the following questionnaire.

7-DAY FOOD DIARY QUESTIONNAIRE: KNOW YOUR TROUBLE SPOTS

I. FOOD AND CALORIES

Look over your food diary and try to calculate how many calories you consumed on an average day. Tough assignment? Yes, it is. But it's also an important one. Although I don't believe in counting each and every calorie, it's necessary for you to have a basic knowledge of the calories in the foods you consume. By calculating your calories, you will also develop some idea of what will be required in order to lose weight.

So, even though it's a tough assignment and your estimates will not be 100 percent accurate, try to calculate your daily caloric intake. (If you don't have a good calorie guide at hand, you may want to invest in one.)

During the period of time covered by my food diary, my average daily calorie intake was _____ .

Keeping in mind that the average weight-loss diet ranges from 1200 to 1800 calories a day (depending on sex, body size, and other factors), I will have to cut my daily intake by about _____ calories to lose weight.

II. FOOD AND NUTRITION

Calories alone can't tell the whole nutrition story. Look back over your diary and ask yourself how well you nourished your body.

Here are some questions to answer.

The percentage of fats in my diet is

_____ too high _____ about right _____ too low

The percentage of protein in my diet is

_____ too high _____ about right _____ too low

The percentage of complex carbohydrates in my diet is

_____ too high _____ about right _____ too low

The percentage of refined carbohydrates in my diet is

_____ too high _____ about right _____ too low

The amount of fresh fruit in my diet is

_____ too high _____ about right _____ too low

The amount of fresh vegetables in my diet is

_____ too high _____ about right _____ too low

The amount of lean meat in my diet is

_____ too high _____ about right _____ too low

The amount of dairy products in my diet is

_____ too high _____ about right _____ too low

The amount of whole grains and cereals in my diet is

_____ too high _____ about right _____ too low

Foods I eat that have little or no nutritional value are:

_____   _____   _____

_____   _____   _____

_____   _____   _____

Other comments:

_____

_____

_____

If you do not know what constitutes a nutritionally sound diet or cannot answer some of these questions, please take time to make yourself an informed consumer. Almost every bookstore and library has a wealth of books on and about nutrition. In addition, the U.S. Department of Agriculture's Food and Nutrition Service publishes a number of pamphlets on the subject. These pamphlets are available through various government bookstores, as well as through the Department of Agriculture in Washington, D.C.

III. FOOD AND BEHAVIOR

Below you'll find a detailed list of inappropriate eating habits. Mark all that applied to you at least once during your recorded week.
Did you

_____ Eat when you weren't hungry?

_____ Eat because the clock said it was time to?

_____ Eat because the sight, scent, or anticipated taste of food stimulated your appetite?

_____ Eat something simply because "it was there"?

_____ Eat to keep someone else company?

_____ Eat to postpone some unpleasant task?

_____ Eat because you were at a social dinner, party, or other affair?

_____ Eat because you wanted to reward yourself?

_____ Eat because you wanted to celebrate something?

_____ Eat because you wanted to prolong your happiness?

_____ Eat because you were bored?

_____ Eat because you were lonely?

_____ Eat because you felt hopeless?

_____ Eat to cheer yourself up?

_____ Eat out of stress or anxiety?

_____ Eat because you were angry?

_____ Eat because you were frustrated?

_____ Eat to show that no one can tell you what to do?

_____ Eat while shopping for food?

_____ Eat on the way home from the grocery store?

_____ Eat while unpacking groceries?

_____ Eat while preparing food?

_____ Eat while serving food?

_____ Eat while doing other kitchen work?

_____ Eat while walking?

_____ Eat standing up?

_____ Eat at your desk while continuing to work?

_____ Eat while engaged in a boring or unpleasant task, like cleaning, doing your taxes, etc. ?

_____ Eat while watching television?

_____ Eat while reading?

_____ Eat while talking on the phone?

_____ Eat in your car?

_____ Eat standing at the refrigerator?

_____ Eat too many snacks?

_____ Eat before bed?

_____ Eat in bed?

_____ Eat in the middle of the night?

_____ Eat at inappropriate times (such as just before dinner, etc.)?

_____ Eat more than you intended to?

_____ Eat more than your body needed?

_____ Overeat to the point of physical discomfort?

_____ Continue to eat even though you were no longer hungry?

_____ Take oversize helpings?

_____ Take second helpings?

_____ Eat from appetite rather than true hunger?

_____ Eat "hoarded" food—that is, items you stashed away to eat in private?

_____ Binge eat?

_____ Eat poorly balanced meals?

_____ Eat high-calorie foods?

_____ Overeat particular foods? List the food or foods:

_____   _____   _____

_____   _____   _____

_____   _____   _____

_____ Eat too quickly?

_____ Eat leftovers you'd intended to save or throw away?

_____ Eat until everything was gone?

_____ Eat to prolong the pleasure of sitting at the table?

_____ Eat because the taste of food was still in your mouth?

_____ Eat while putting food away?

_____ Eat while doing dishes or cleaning up the kitchen?

Other:

_____ _____

_____ _____

_____ _____

_____ _____

_____ _____

_____ _____

_____ _____

_____ _____

_____ _____

Can you see what's happening here? The eating problem you thought was large, complex, uncontrollable and even hopeless a week ago is nothing more than a combination of bad habits and inappropriate responses.

When tackling a weight problem, many overeaters want to look for deep insights and psychological revelations. If you are someone who eats to cope with his or her emotional problems, therapy may be an appropriate track to take. For most people, however, the answer is much simpler. It lies in *behavior modification*—changing the patterns and habits that led them to put on excess weight in the first place.

For each trouble spot targeted by the questionnaire, there is at least one simple success strategy. Usually, there are two, three, or more such strategies, any or all of which can be used to change the habit. You don't need to be a psychiatrist or physician to discover these behavior-altering strategies. You—an intelligent, motivated person—are more than qualified to devise your own success strategies from the ideas and techniques presented in this book.

Remember that everything you read throughout these pages is based on real people's experiences. What I have learned through working with my patients can now be put to work for you.

How can this work for you? Let's say that you have a hard time putting food away without continuing to snack on it. You've identified your problem, and that's half the battle. Don't make your problem worse by telling yourself that you should learn to put food away without eating it, or by comparing yourself to others who can do this. Putting food away is a problem for you, just as liquor is a problem for an alcoholic. You wouldn't tell an alcoholic bartender to "learn" to ignore his environment, would you? No, you'd advise him to *change the situation.*

That's what you need to do for yourself. How can you change the "putting food away" situation so that it will no longer be a trouble spot?

Well, if you live in a family or with others, you might trade tasks with someone: If another person will put the food away, you will do something for him in return. If you live alone, you could put the extra food away *before* sitting down to eat. (Putting it in the freezer will really help you avoid temptation.)

Or you could short-circuit temptation by preparing *only* as much food as you have decided to eat at the meal. The idea of making a double serving in order to have leftovers may be efficient and economical—but not if the leftovers end up on your thighs! A third strategy might be to make sure the only leftovers are healthy ones, like raw vegetables from the salad. Or you might save part of your meal—a piece of fruit, for example—to snack on as you clean up.

Finding out exactly what works for you will take a bit of experimentation, but simple and direct strategies like this are almost always more successful and much less stressful than browbeating yourself with ideas about what you *should* and *shouldn't* do.

If you have completed the 7-Day Food Diary questionnaire you have a good idea of where your trouble spots lie. On pages 150–151 you will find a Success Strategy Worksheet. For each trouble spot, come up with at least one strategy (and preferably two or three) that you will use in conjunction with your diet. You probably won't have any trouble finding simple and creative ways to change your behavior, but here are some ideas to get you started. Write down the ones that appeal to you or alter them to accommodate your individual interests and needs.

- Use the Touch-Control Method before deciding to eat.
- Use the Stoplines to determine true hunger.
- Use the self-hypnosis techniques you learned on Day 5 to cope with stress and tension.
- Before deciding to eat, have a glass of water and think it over.
- Do not eat until your *body* tells you it's time to eat.
- If you must keep other eaters company (at a lunch appointment, dinner date, etc.) and are not hungry, drink club soda or eat only a salad.
- Decide to have only a certain number of snacks each day.
- Change television or radio channels to avoid tempting food commercials.
- Change your usual route to avoid walking by delicatessen, candy store, or other place that triggers your appetite.

- Develop a list of nonfood rewards.
- Develop a "things to do" list to keep yourself busy. Avoid boredom at all costs.
- Involve yourself in activities and interests outside yourself and your diet. Join a club, take up a hobby, volunteer.
- When you are lonely, call, write, or visit a friend.
- When you are angry, write a letter to the person who's making you angry. You don't have to mail it, but you *do* have to express your feelings in a way that doesn't involve eating.
- When you are frustrated, ask yourself what you can do to improve the situation for yourself.
- When you buy groceries, put them in the trunk or back seat of your car on the way home, or have them delivered.
- Unpack and put away all groceries without opening any items.
- Prepare foods that don't invite snacking during the cooking process, like broiled chicken.
- Eliminate foods that require involved preparation and invite snacking, like slow-simmered spaghetti sauce or other foods you find particularly tempting.
- Reduce the chances of "unconscious" eating by deciding to eat at one and only one designated place in your house.
- Decide not to eat in bed, standing up, at the kitchen counter, or other places where you tend to consume unnecessary, unplanned snacks.
- Decide not to eat in conjunction with other activities, like watching television, reading, working, studying, etc. Remember that when you eat, all of your attention should be on eating.
- Each morning, make a food plan for the day and stick to it as closely as possible.
- Each morning, plan what time you will have your meals that day. This will help you stick to you diet and avoid snacks that aren't on your meal plan.
- Learn to cook low-calorie recipes.

- Prepare only as much food as will be eaten at any one meal.
- Eliminate binge foods from your home.
- If you live with others who must have "temptation" foods on hand, store these foods out of sight, in the freezer, in closed, nontransparent jars, or in the most inconvenient place you can think of.
- Create a beautiful and relaxed eating environment to get the most enjoyment out of each meal.
- Put the amount of food you intend to eat on your plate. No second helpings, please!
- Concentrate on eating slowly and fully enjoying your meal.
- If you are full before your food is finished, learn to leave the uneaten food on your plate.
- Wait fifteen minutes before going ahead and taking a second helping. This is about how long it will take your stomach to signal your brain that you are full.
- Remove leftovers from the table as soon as possible—then relax and enjoy the candlelight and conversation.
- Don't save leftover food if it will tempt you to overeat. Throw it away instead or freeze it for future use.
- Make sure all food is put away before beginning any kitchen work.

All right, I think you get the idea. These strategies are general (you may have heard some of them before), but they will work for you if you make them *personal* and *specific*. For instance, if you're going to ask your husband to take care of the leftovers so you won't have to deal with them, write "trade kitchen cleanup with Bob in exchange for washing car." If you are going to head off boredom by expanding your horizons, have a concrete idea of how you will go about that: a pottery class at the Y, jazzercise classes, or joining the Literacy Volunteers. Once you start looking into the possibilities, you'll wonder how you ever found time to lie around the house and eat!

Now devise your own strategies for success.

SUCCESS STRATEGY WORKSHEET

1. _____

2. _____

3. _____

4. _____

5. _____

6. _____

7. _____

8. _____

9. _____

10. _____

11. _____

12. _____

13. _____

14. _____

15. _____

16. _____

17. _____

18. _____

19. _____

20. _____

The Power of Self-Talk

What kind of messages do you give yourself every day? When you catch your reflection in a store window do you respond with a negative comment to yourself? When you eat more than you intend do you rationalize by telling yourself that *no one* could resist something so delicious? When you go on a diet do you expect yourself to fail because "that's the kind of person I am"?

All of these are examples of self-talk, the internal dialogue we engage in with ourselves throughout the day. This self-talk can be either positive or negative. I like to compare self-talk to computer programming. If you compare the human brain to a computer, you have to admit that the brain is probably the best and most effective computer there is. It can learn an enormous amount of new information and its storage capacity is vast.

So make use of this storage capacity and program your "brain-computer" with positive messages and images about your body and the way you relate to it.

Are you ready to try this?

(Your answer) _____

For example, instead of saying to yourself, "I hate my body, it's so out of shape and ugly" (a negative message), give yourself a positive message such as,

"My poor body is trying its best in spite of my constant overfeeding of it. Starting today, I will try to take care of my body in a more attentive and protective way. As a result of this, my body will start shedding all the extra weight it has put on."

Here's another example of replacing negative programming with positive programming. Instead of saying, "No sense in dieting today—I ate so much yesterday I've blown my diet completely," reprogram your thinking with this positive statement: "Dear body, forgive me for having stuffed you with too much food yesterday. I will not repeat this abuse again today. Today I will feed you right and take good care of you."

Take a moment to think about the kind of self-talk you engage in with yourself about your body and your eating habits. Is it generally positive or negative?

(Your answer) _____

Notice that even though rationalization and denial aren't overtly critical, they are negative because they are self-destructive.

Use the space below to give some examples of your negative self-talk.

_____

_____

_____

_____

_____

_____

_____

_____

Use this space to give examples of your positive self-talk.

_____

_____

_____

_____

_____

_____

_____

_____

If you're like many people, you had an easier time filling the first set of blanks than the second set. It's always amazing and distressing to see how many wonderful, loving people have trouble loving and appreciating themselves.

Where does the self-talk come from? If you look carefully, you'll probably see that at least some of it echoes a parental voice you heard in childhood. "Harry is our little butterball," say Harry's parents, and Harry learns to think of himself as a butterball for life. "If only you'd lose weight," nags Catherine's mother, "I'm sure someone would ask you to the dance." Twenty years later, Catherine still sees herself as someone excluded from life because of the extra weight she carries.

Other messages come from the world around us: the media, our friends, our mates, our children. The husband who constantly nags his wife about her weight may think he is helping by acting as her conscience. The truth is that he is not helping at all. He is teaching his wife to think of herself as fat and is creating a stressful situation that will encourage her to eat more, not less.

Despite all of this, *you* are responsible for the self-talk that goes on inside your head. You *can* take control of it. If you are burdened with negative, self-deprecating messages, you can *replace* them with positive, esteem-building messages.

How?

Begin by freeing yourself of the negative self-talk you have adopted. It's really a very simple process.

- *Step 1.* Identify the negative or sabotaging message in your head. If it's a feeling or an assumption you've never expressed, put it into words. "No one will love me until I lose weight" and "I'm a bad person with no willpower—I don't deserve to be thin" are two common beliefs of overweight people.

- *Step 2.* Take responsibility. Don't blame your critical parents or anyone else in the outside world for giving you this negative message. Wherever it came from initially, you have chosen to make it part of your self-talk. Acknowledge that by saying, "I use this statement (or belief) to beat myself up and keep myself stuck in a negative situation."

- *Step 3.* Disown the message. You can do this in a few ways. One is to exaggerate the message in order to see how ridiculous and untrue it really is. If you believe that "No one will love me until I lose weight," go on to state exactly what that would mean if it were true: "That's right. Because I need to lose weight, I have no real friends. The people who seem to care for me are only pretending out of pity. They do not really enjoy my company at all. No one of the opposite sex has ever found me attractive. I have never had a date in my life and will undoubtedly die a virgin. It's true: Being thin is all that counts in love."

Another way to disown the negative message is through action. When the message comes to mind, turn it off by occupying yourself with something else instead. Pick up a book, complete a task, or put on some clothes that make you feel attractive.

The third, most direct, and best way to disown the negative message is to replace it with a positive and helpful one. Instead of believing that you're a bad person with no willpower, tell yourself the truth: You are a good person, you deserve the body you want, and you are moving closer to that goal every single day.

Changing Negative to Positive

Not all of the negative self-talk that goes on in your head has to do with your self-image, and not all of it comes from critical outside forces. Some negative beliefs are the result of your own confused thinking. Misconceptions, denial, perfectionism, procrastination, and wishful thinking all conspire to keep you stuck in a layer of fat. Below are some key areas to focus on as you move closer to Take-Off Day. Be honest in identifying your own destructive attitudes. Be courageous in getting ready to face life without these excuses and cop-outs. Most of all, be loving and positive as you replace each negative belief with its positive alternative.

Food

Unlike an alcoholic or drug addict, you do not have the luxury of simply giving up the substance that causes you trouble. You will have to face food every single day for the rest of your life. Because of this, your attitude towards food is very important.

Here are some destructive ideas people have about food:

- Food is my enemy.
- Food is bad. It makes me fat.
- Food is my lover and my best friend.

- Certain foods are irresistible.
- Food should make me happy.
- Food should always be satisfying.

Use this space to write down your destructive ideas about food:

_____

_____

_____

_____

_____

Now change your destructive, erroneous beliefs to positive and helpful ones. Here are a few examples to get you going:

- Food is neither my enemy nor my lover; it is only food.
- I am able to resist foods that are poisonous to my body.
- Not all meals are satisfying and that is all right with me.
- I have come to recognize that not all meals are equally important.

_____

_____

_____

_____

_____

Dieting

Here are some destructive ideas people have about dieting:

- Dieting is painful and serious.
- Dieting is punishment and deprivation.
- The reward of staying on a diet is getting to eat again.
- Dieting should be easy.

Use this space to write down your destructive ideas about dieting:

_____

_____

_____

_____

_____

Now change your destructive, erroneous beliefs to positive and helpful ones. Here are a few examples to get you going:

- Dieting is something I chose to do for myself.
- Dieting is the wonderful tool that will help me reach my goal.
- Dieting can be liberating.
- Dieting can be uncomfortable, but I will endure the discomfort to reach my goal.

_____

_____

_____

_____

_____

_____

Your Eating Behavior

To achieve your goal and maintain it, it is essential to change your beliefs about your eating patterns. We have already done some work with "thin" and "fat" eating. Now let's do a bit more. Notice that I've left extra space for you to examine this important issue. (If it isn't enough, add paper of your own.)

Here are some destructive ideas people have about eating behavior:

- I'm always hungry.
- Once I start eating, I can't stop.
- I can't stay on a diet because I always give in to temptation.
- I can lose weight, but I can't keep it off because food is too alluring to me.

Use this space to write down your destructive ideas about your eating patterns:

_____

_____

_____

_____

_____

_____

_____

_____

_____

_____

Now change your destructive, erroneous beliefs to positive and helpful ones. Here are a few examples to get you going:

- I eat only when my body is truly hungry.
- I often have appetite cravings but I am strong enough to resist them.
- Armed with motivation and the techniques this book has taught me, I am now able to lose weight.

_____

_____

_____

_____

_____

_____

_____

_____

_____

_____

Your Body

No matter what its size or shape, your body deserves to be treated well. Only through caring for your body, appreciating it, and wanting to act in its best interests will you be able to feed it correctly. Only through loving yourself as you are will you achieve true contentment.

Here are some destructive ideas people have about their bodies:

- My body has nothing to do with the "real" me.
- My body is my enemy because it gains weight.
- My body is my shield against reality.
- My body is weak, sagging, and ugly.
- My body does not deserve praise, love, or admiration.

Use this space to write down your destructive ideas about your body.

_____

_____

_____

_____

_____

_____

_____

_____

_____

_____

Now change your destructive, erroneous beliefs to positive and helpful ones. Here are a few examples to get you going:

- My body is my instrument for living.
- My body is an expression of my interior self.
- My body is vulnerable and deserves full attention and protection.
- My body is my friend. It follows my commands and houses my soul.
- My body is, as any living creature, nature's creation and work of art.

_____

_____

_____

_____

_____

_____

_____

_____

_____

_____

As you diet, focus often on these positive beliefs. Read them every morning and every evening. Even if they don't seem right to you at first, you will come to see that they are true. As these positive messages replace the negative ones you formerly lived by, you will see your behavior altering to fit them. You will begin to act in ways that are healthy, positive, productive, and loving.

Now, before today's work is finished, repeat out loud this true statement about yourself:

Every day, by working in a positive and dedicated way, I am getting closer to my goal. I will let nothing stand between myself and achievement. I have worked hard and will continue to work hard. I deserve to be slim and healthy.

If you felt a bit boastful or uncomfortable as you read, read the statement out loud again. Don't shy away from it. It's absolutely true. You have completed eight days of the 10-day diet countdown. You've armed yourself with techniques and strategies to keep your motivation going strong. Your goal is at hand and you will achieve it.

DAY NINE

REWARD DAY

Today's the day to:

- Create a Rewards List.
- Establish a Wish List and Bank Account.
- Create an Alternate Activities List.

DON'T BE alarmed by the abundance of blank spaces in this chapter! I promise that you won't have to do any uncomfortable soul searching. Nor will you have to keep an inventory of the food you eat. You've completed the hard work of the 10-day diet countdown and today and tomorrow are going to be fun and enjoyable for you.

Today you're going to begin choosing items and activities that will take the place of food and help you toward your goal. If your life has been so crowded with food that there hasn't been room for anything else, today's the day to expand your horizons. When you say goodbye to overeating, you create new spaces in your life for pleasure, experiences, and accomplishments.

Are you ready to begin this adventure?

(Your answer) _____

Let's go!

Nonfood Rewards

No matter what anyone tells you, dieting is work. It requires patience, perseverance, and no small degree of courage. As you diet, it's very important to reinforce yourself with rewards along the way. Of course, the slimmer body you achieve will be a reward, but I want you to give yourself other rewards as well.

In the past, you may have used food as a reward. Many of us do. But now that you've decided to stop using food as a reward, what are you going to give yourself instead?

A lot of people draw a blank here. They have a hard time patting themselves on the back and an even harder time giving to themselves in a positive way. To help you get going, I've outlined some things that might lead to making your life richer in any number of ways. You probably won't be able to fill in all the blanks just now. In fact, if you are not used to rewarding yourself in ways that don't include eating, you may find this task downright difficult. But do it anyway, because you're worth rewarding, whether you believe it or not. Then, as you think of other rewards to give yourself, come back and add to your list. If you run out of room, use your own sheet of paper—there's no such thing as a list that's too long!

Be sure to come back to this list and use it when you begin your diet. Each time you find yourself struggling with a food craving, each time you successfully resist the urge to eat, each time you do the right thing for your body and move closer to your goal, reward yourself with one of the items on the list!

MY REWARDS LIST

Items or activities that will make me feel cared for (for example, having a manicure, buying sexy underwear, or treating myself to a new haircut):

1. _____

2. _____

3. _____

4. _____

5. _____

6. _____

Items or activities that will make me feel more successful about my job or career (for example, keeping my desk organized, or writing all those overdue letters and reports):

1. _____

2. _____

3. _____

4. _____

5. _____

6. _____

Items or activities that will make me feel better about the place in which I live (for example, having fresh flowers in the living room, or treating myself to some relaxing music as soon as I get home):

1. _____

2. _____

3. _____

4. _____

5. _____

6. _____

Items or activities that will make me laugh (for example, spending time with my children, watching a funny movie, or reading a funny book):

1. _____

2. _____

3. _____

4. _____

5. _____

6. _____

Items or activities that will enrich my relationship with my partner (for example, setting aside some private time to talk about our day or exchanging love letters):

1. _____

2. _____

3. _____

4. _____

5. _____

6. _____

Items or activities that will enrich my relationship with my children (for example, taking turns making up stories about ourselves or cuddling more):

1. _____

2. _____

3. _____

4. _____

5. _____

6. _____

Items or activities that will enrich my relationship with my parents and/or siblings (for example, creating a family video or taking a vacation together):

1. _____

2. _____

3. _____

4. _____

5. _____

6. _____

Items or activities that will enrich my relationship with my friends (for example, remembering friends' birthdays and anniversaries or sharing a summer house with friends):

1. _____

2. _____

3. _____

4. _____

5. _____

6. _____

Items or activities that will make me feel more relaxed (for example, meditating daily or organizing my time better):

1. _____

2. _____

3. _____

4. _____

5. _____

6. _____

Items or activities that will make me feel more attractive (for example, buying a new flattering dress or jacket—something I feel good in at any weight):

1. _____

2. _____

3. _____

4. _____

5. _____

6. _____

Items or activities that will make me feel sexier (for example, buying some sexy lingerie or sharing a fantasy with someone close):

1. _____

2. _____

3. _____

4. _____

5. _____

6. _____

Items or activities that will make me healthier (for example, quitting smoking or walking somewhere rather than driving):

1. _____

2. _____

3. _____

4. _____

5. _____

6. _____

Items or activities that will make me a more interesting or better-informed person (for example, reading a newspaper every day or making it a point to meet new people):

1. _____

2. _____

3. _____

4. _____

5. _____

6. _____

Ways I can express myself creatively (for example, redecorating a room in my home or writing an article for my local newspaper):

1. _____

2. _____

3. _____

4. _____

5. _____

6. _____

Things I would like to learn about or activities I would like to learn to do (for example, learning to paint or learning how to drive a stick-shift car):

1. _____

2. _____

3. _____

4. _____

5. _____

6. _____

Items or activities that will help me think of myself as a thin person (for example, visualizing myself thin in different situations or learning to eat like a thin person):

1. _____

2. _____

3. _____

4. _____

5. _____

6. _____

Steps I can take to feel in control of my life (for example, being financially independent of my family or learning how to say no when I mean no):

1. _____

2. _____

3. _____

4. _____

5. _____

6. _____

Ways I can make the world a better place (for example, deciding not to litter and not letting my friends or family litter, or volunteering my time where it is needed):

1. _____

2. _____

3. _____

4. _____

5. _____

6. _____

Additional:

1. _____

2. _____

3. _____

4. _____

5. _____

6. _____

Wish Lists and Bank Accounts

There's no doubt about it: It takes money to stay overweight. Groceries costs money, and fattening items—doughnuts, fast food, and the like—are amazingly expensive. When you reach Take-Off Day and give up these expensive goodies, you're going to have some extra money on your hands.

What are you going to do with it?

It's important to acknowledge your savings in some way. If you are single, you can redirect the bonus money to something just for you. If you are married, you may choose to channel the money into something you want for your family.

As you diet, keep a wish list of things you want. They can be anything from the trivial—like new eye shadow, to the substantial—like a family vacation. Every time you forgo an expensive snack or food item, record the money you save. This is money to put toward items on your wish list. Even if you can't save enough to afford the larger items, your savings can make an important contribution!

WISH LIST AND PERSONAL BANK ACCOUNT

THINGS I WOULD LIKE

Item   Cost

_____   _____

_____   _____

_____   _____

_____   _____

_____   _____

_____   _____

_____   _____

_____   _____

_____   _____

_____   _____

_____   _____

MY BANK ACCOUNT

Food Item Not Bought	Cost	Previous Balance	CURRENT BALANCE
_____	_____ +	_____ =	_____
_____	_____ +	_____ =	_____
_____	_____ +	_____ =	_____
_____	_____ +	_____ =	_____
_____	_____ +	_____ =	_____
_____	_____ +	_____ =	_____
_____	_____ +	_____ =	_____
_____	_____ +	_____ =	_____

Learning to Do

Rewarding yourself is a good, positive thing to do, but it shouldn't be the whole focus of your weight-loss program. There's something to be said for plain old work as well.

Are you someone who has used eating to put off tasks that need to be attended to? If so, now's the time to get them done. Leaving things undone encourages an "out of control" feeling, and this feeling can lead you right back to the refrigerator.

Start a list of tasks to do and begin *doing* them. The work itself—replacing a button on your coat, putting your correspondence in order, or making an appointment for new eyeglasses—may not be fun, but the feeling of accomplishment that will come to you will be well worth the effort. As the days go by and you take care of business instead of avoiding it with food, you will be establishing a new and positive behavior pattern.

ALTERNATE ACTIVITIES LIST

Task: Date Completed:

1. _____   _____

2. _____   _____

3. _____   _____

4. _____   _____

5. _____   _____

6. _____   _____

7. _____   _____

8. _____   _____

9. _____   _____

10. _____   _____

11. _____   _____

12. _____   _____

13. _____   _____

14. _____   _____

15. _____   _____

Learning to Feel Good Without Food

Hard to imagine feeling good without food? It's possible. In fact, it's a feeling you should enjoy often. To get into the habit, pick one thing from your Rewards List or from your Alternate Activities List and make it today's gift to yourself. Enjoy it, because of the pleasure it brings, or because of the sense of accomplishment that goes with it. Remember: *you deserve it!*

DAY TEN

FINAL TUNE-UP DAY

Today's the day to:

- Give up one of your "problem" foods.
- Eat a practice meal.
- Fat-proof your environment.
- Resupply your kitchen.

YOU'RE ONLY twenty-four hours away from Take-Off Day. You may think the hard work is about to begin, but this isn't really true. Your journey began more than a week ago when you picked up this book. The work you've done in that time has already brought you closer to your goal of losing weight. This time, instead of going on a diet "cold turkey," you are prepared. In your mind, you have already begun to think like a thin person.

Today, you are going to practice that way of thinking and feeling. Let's begin with your usual morning routine. I would like you to describe what you do in the first half hour you are awake—your normal dressing, hygiene, and eating habits.

What is your normal pattern?

_____

_____

_____

_____

Many people don't take time for themselves in the morning. They tumble out of bed, attend to the basics, and reach blindly for the first food that meets their eye. Or they skip breakfast completely—a habit that often leads to hunger, exhaustion, and the temptation to binge at midmorning. If this is the routine you've fallen into, it's time to change it.

Take time for yourself in the morning. Stretch. Take an extra minute to enjoy the fact that you are alive and well. Take another thirty seconds to make a contract with your body: *Today, I will feed my body only foods that are good for it.* Do something that makes you feel physically attractive, like wearing your favorite earrings or giving your shoes a quick buff. Before you jump headlong into your day, put yourself in a relaxed, positive frame of mind by practicing the self-hypnosis technique you learned on Day 5.

Please don't say you don't have time for these things—at most, these suggestions will take five to seven minutes. Aren't you worth this much attention:

(Your answer) _____

Taking time for yourself each morning is important. It allows you a "breathing space" in which to remember your goals and think about your priorities. It's a way of taking control of your life, and control is what healthy eating is all about.

Practicing

By now, having kept a detailed food diary, you have a good idea of the foods that give you trouble. Sweets, salty foods, and high-fat or high-carbohydrate items are the usual culprits because they are easily accessible and because they satisfy appetite rather than true hunger. Remember, however, that almost any food can be a "trouble food" if you binge on it.

What are *your* trouble foods?

_____

_____

_____

_____

_____

Today, you are going to practice thin eating by giving up one of these foods. As the day goes on, notice how many times you want this food and how you feel about not having it. Use the techniques you have learned (such as Stoplines and Supportlines, self-hypnosis, and alternative rewards) to help you through the day, and use the space below to record your feelings and reactions. Writing exercises like this will help you see clearly the role a particular food has come to play in your life. They will also provide you with information about what support techniques work best for you.

ON GIVING UP A FAVORED FOOD

How I felt without this food:

_____

_____

_____

_____

_____

The techniques I practiced:

_____

_____

_____

_____

Activities I substituted for eating:

_____

_____

_____

_____

_____

Rewards I gave myself:

_____

_____

_____

_____

_____

There's another thing for you to do today, and that's to practice eating. Yes, I know—when it comes to eating you already consider yourself quite an expert.

But are you?

You're probably an expert at fat eating—eating to satisfy appetite rather than true hunger. When it comes to eating for nutrition's sake, you're a novice. You have to learn to feed yourself all over again.

Do you have a thin friend, one of those people who "can eat anything and not gain a pound"? Well, some people do have metabolism on their side. But most people who maintain a healthy weight can't get away with overeating any more than the rest of us. If you watched them eat, you would learn a lot. You would learn how to become a thin eater for life.

Below is a list of principles you will need to follow to become a thin eater. Today, I want you to follow them as you eat a practice meal. Do you think you can do that?

(Your answer) _____

Good. Let's eat.

Rules for Thin Eating

- *Do not eat unless you are truly hungry.* No matter how good the food looks, no matter who else is eating around you—if you aren't really hungry, *don't eat!*
- *Eat sitting down.* Not standing up, not on the run, not in the car, not in bed.
- *Eat in the most relaxed atmosphere possible.* Even if you have clamoring children to feed, make your meal an enjoyable experience. Set an unhurried tone or experiment with feeding the children first.
- *Don't allow yourself to be distracted while you are eating.* Eating is not an accompaniment for television, telephone, reading, or working.
- *Decide what to eat.* Don't eat something simply because it's there. Carefully choose the food you will eat and take full responsibility for its nutritional content.
- *Be grateful for the food you are about to eat.* Saying grace is never out of place. Remember, food nourishes your body and you need your body to live.
- *Practice portion control.* Be aware of how much food you are putting on your plate. Measure your portions until, with practice, you can estimate accurately.
- *Don't eat anything that isn't on your plate.*
- *Chew your food well.* Taste and savor every bite. It is only in your mouth that you truly taste food. Once in your stomach, you have no taste experience.
- *Don't feel guilty about eating.* Many overweight people have been giving themselves "don't eat" messages for so long they feel they should feel guilty over every bite. However, there's no reason to feel guilty about putting nutritious food into your body. Remember, guilt leads to confusion, depression, and bingeing.
- *Swallow your food before you put the next bite into your mouth.* I know you've probably heard this before, but do it anyway. The reason you've heard it so often is because it works.
- *Eat slowly.* Give your stomach and brain time to register fullness.

- *Don't take second helpings.* If you want more, wait fifteen minutes. Allow the food to reach your stomach before deciding whether or not you need more.
- *Stop eating as soon you are satisfied.* No matter how good the food tastes, no matter how much is left on your plate or how little you have eaten, *stop* when your hunger eases.
- *After you finish, remain seated.* Prolong the enjoyable relaxation break a meal provides without continuing to eat. This is the time to listen to some music or talk to your mate. Even young children can be taught to respect these few minutes of "grown-up time."

Now record your thoughts and feelings about this new way of eating. Was it hard for you, or easy? Did you discover any resistance within yourself? Did you feel your eating was in control?

_____

_____

_____

_____

_____

_____

_____

_____

As you diet, consciously follow the rules on this list until they become an automatic part of your eating behavior.

Fat-Proof Your Environment

The world is full of eating cues: commercials that promise pizza delivery in thirty minutes, store windows bursting with salami and cheese, the office coffee cart whose bell announces the arrival of butter, rolls, and Danishes.

How are you going to avoid temptation?

One of the best ways is simply to avoid coming into contact with the cues. There's a lot to be said about the old adage, "Out of sight, out of mind." Today, take a good look at your environment and see what you can do to keep out of harm's—or, in this case, fat's—way.

To get you started, here are some common pitfalls and how to work around them:

• *Your kitchen.* Don't leave food in sight if you can possibly avoid it. Canisters brimming with flour and sugar may make you want to bake. Glass jars of pasta may spell c-a-r-b-o-n-a-r-a. The ultimate disaster is the cookie jar. Even an empty one stimulates your appetite.

• *The cupboards.* What do you see when you open your cupboards? Make sure anything that might tempt you is far to the back or in an opaque container. Fill the front rows with spices, the vinegar, and Worcestershire sauce bottles.

• *The refrigerator.* Throw out any food that you won't be eating tomorrow. Do it today when you aren't hungry, at a time when you're feeling strong. If you don't live alone and must keep "problem" foods on hand for others, make sure these foods are out of sight. Store foods in foil and opaque dishes rather than in plastic wrap. Rearrange the fridge with *you* in mind: Keep butter, cheese, and other high-calorie items in the vegetable crisper and keep your vegetables—trimmed and ready for snacking—in plain view.

• *Your house.* I once had a patient who complained of craving chocolate-chip cookies whenever she visited a particular friend. It turned out that the friend scented her home with vanilla candles, and the aroma reminded my patient of the cookies her mother used to bake. Is your house scented with apple, rum raisin, orange, cinnamon, or blueberry? Switch your candles and potpourri to florals or eucalyptus.

- *Beauty products.* Soap, hair products, skin creams, and other beauty products can read like a menu. Coconut, avocado, peach, and almond are only a few of the scents you're likely to encounter. I once had a patient who told me her cocoa-butter body lotion smelled exactly like chocolate-covered dough-nuts! Sniff you way through your toiletries and eliminate anything that might appeal to your imagination.

- *The television.* A vast number of television commercials are designed to sell food. Why do these commercials continue to air? Because they work. They make you desire and eventually buy foods you ordinarily wouldn't be aware of. If you have a remote control, keep it near you whenever you watch television. When the next tempting food commercial comes on, zap it.

- *The outside world.* Does your daily route lead you past fast-food restau-rants, bakeries, or other temptations? See if there's anything you can do to alter your path. Maybe you can park in a different spot or walk on the opposite side of the street. Remember, it's always easier to keep a craving from happening than to wrestle with it once it's in full flower.

Use the spaces below to list the eating cues you encounter daily. Then devise strategies for avoiding them. Remember, an avoidance strategy doesn't have to be complex; it just has to be effective.

- _____

_____

_____

_____

- _____

_____

_____

_____

- _____

_____

_____

_____

- _____

_____

_____

_____

Restocking Your Kitchen

Once you have eliminated as many temptations from your environment as possible, you must get ready to feed yourself right. This means preparing *in advance* for Take-Off Day.

The first task you will have to do is go shopping. The grocery store is a veritable tar pit of temptation for most people. Every aisle is bursting with delicious food and, unless you are wealthy enough to have a maid or lucky enough to have a husband or a friend who will shop for you, you will have to learn to navigate your way through these hazardous waters without swamping your diet.

Here are some tips that will help you:

- *Plan what to buy.* Never go shopping without a list and never buy anything that isn't on your list.
- *Plan when to shop.* For years people have been told never to shop when they are hungry. However, a recent study indicates that overweight people will buy more food when they are full, possibly because eating has put them in a good mood and they want to "celebrate" their happiness with groceries. Observe your own shopping patterns to determine when is your best time to buy food.
- *Plan where to shop.* Since your diet will probably be high in fresh fruits and vegetables, you may want to do as much shopping as possible at your local greengrocer. Not only will you be likely to get better quality produce, you will not be assaulted with the temptations of a large grocery store.
- *Don't go down every aisle.* Fortunately for the health-conscious, grocery stores do have a rhyme and reason to them. Fruits and vegetables are in one aisle, canned goods in another, and so on. You'll discover that there are at least parts of aisles—the brownie and cake mix shelf, for example—that you can skip altogether.

Now, are you ready to face the grocery store? With your diet plan in front of you, make a shopping list for the first few days, remembering that some items (meat, certain fruits, and vegetables) will lose their taste appeal if they are purchased too many days in advance.

GROCERY LIST

_____   _____

_____   _____

_____   _____

_____   _____

_____   _____

_____   _____

_____   _____

_____   _____

_____   _____

_____   _____

_____   _____

_____   _____

_____   _____

_____   _____

_____   _____

Each Day of Your Diet

On each day of your diet, look ahead to see what you will be eating tomorrow. Does your lunch call for a sandwich of cold roast chicken? If you are cooking your own food, bake the chicken tonight so that your lunch will be ready and waiting when you need it.

The same kind of advance planning and preparation is necessary when it comes to fruits and vegetables. One of the reasons people reach for chips, crackers, rolls, and cookies when they are hungry is because these snacks are readily available and need no preparation. Healthy food, on the other hand, usually requires washing, peeling, cutting, cooking, and so forth. If you open your refrigerator and see a cantaloupe, the effort of cutting into it and cleaning the seeds may deter you. After all, you're hungry and you want something to eat *right now*. But if you open the refrigerator and see a bowl of melon cubes, you'll be able to reach for them and enjoy them immediately.

One other hint: Celery sticks are great diet food, but if you hate celery, don't fill your refrigerator with it. Look for snacks that are compatible with your taste buds as well as your diet. Almost any raw green or yellow vegetable is a good bet (carrot sticks, green pepper rings, broccoli flowerets, etc.), as is hot bouillon or consommé. Some diets include special snacks such as air-popped popcorn and raw fruit wedges. No matter what you snack on, however, make sure you know its caloric content. Although *most* raw green vegetables are exceptionally healthy, a raw avocado packs a three- or four-hundred-calorie wallop and should be avoided at all costs.

You're Almost There

Did you think you'd make it through these ten days? Maybe you had some doubts about yourself in the beginning or even along the way. But you did it! Here's your certificate of honor for the successful completion of the 10-day diet countdown.

DIPLOMA

I, _____, am a graduate in good standing of the 10-day diet countdown.

I have persevered through the exercises and done my homework.

In return for my effort, I have acquired the tools and learned the techniques that will allow me to become a thin person in body and in mind.

Each day, one day at a time, I have affirmed and strengthened my motivation.

I have worked hard and will continue to work hard. Because of this, I deserve all the happiness my slim, healthy, desirable body will bring me.

Date of graduation: _____

We are now at the end of Day 10, but that doesn't mean this is the last day you and I will spend together. Remember, you will be using this book as a guide each and every day of your diet. To help you, I've included the next section (Take-Off Day) to serve as a reminder and a road map to all that you have learned in the past ten days.

Now let me offer you my personal congratulations. I'm proud of you and I admire your perseverance and motivation. Remember to take good care of yourself from here on out: You're an important person and you deserve the best in life!

TAKE-OFF DAY: A PEP TALK AND REVIEW

THANKS TO the work you've put in during the last ten days, your enthusiasm is high and your motivation is going strong. But how do you keep that motivation up as you diet? By using this book and the techniques in it as a companion and guide. Over the last week and a half you've made *Your Diet Coach* a personal reference book, one you can come back to each and every day of your diet.

Using This Book as You Diet

As they begin to diet, people often ask, "What should I do each day? How many times should I practice the Touch-Control Method? Should I begin the day with self-hypnosis?"

You probably have similar questions.

First of all, remember to be *flexible*. As you no doubt know, life doesn't stop just because you're on a diet, and regimes that are too rigid are almost impossible to follow.

As you diet, *come back to this book often.* If you are having a problem ridding yourself of negative thinking, it will help you to reread the section that deals with that. If you need a motivational boost, there are plenty of ideas between the two covers of this book. Don't make the mistake of thinking that because you have finished reading *Your Diet Coach* and working the exercises, it has nothing more to give you. Each time you reread a section you will be reinforcing your motivation and moving closer toward your goal!

In addition, here are a few guidelines to follow each day of your diet.

Guidelines to Follow

- *Practice the Touch-Control Method (page 61) every time you eat something.* Each time you put food in your mouth, practice the Touch-Control Method first. When this response becomes automatic, you are on your way to a lifetime of healthy eating.

- *Practice self-hypnosis (pages 97–101) several times throughout the day.* Morning is a good time of day to refresh your motivation and bring your goals into focus through self-hypnosis. If this isn't possible for you, look for times in your day that are less rushed: on the way to work if you take mass transit, after the children are in school, in a relaxing moment when you come out of a shower. If you have to face a situation that is problematic—such as a social dinner at which you may be tempted to overeat—practice self-hypnosis beforehand to reinforce your motivation and rehearse your behavior at the upcoming event.

- *Practice visualization (page 114) frequently throughout the day.* Give yourself permission to go on brief "daydream vacations" in which you visualize your goals: a slimmer body, wearing a particular garment in a smaller size, or turning down a favored food without a feeling of loss and deprivation.

- *Practice the Supportlines (page 133) whenever you are tempted to overeat.* The Supportlines are particularly useful in helping you distinguish between true hunger and appetite craving. Use them to turn off cravings that can lead to a binge.

• *Know your danger times.* By now, you have a good idea of the times of the day that spell trouble for you. A good strategy for coping with "the dangerous hours" is to practice your techniques before and during them. If you are an after-work eater, for example, be sure to practice self-hypnosis, visualization, and the Supportlines at the *beginning* of your evening. If you are someone who wakes up in the middle of the night longing to raid the ice box, practice your techniques before bed.

• *Drink plenty of water.* I know it sounds boring—and often it is—but disciplining yourself to drink eight to ten glasses of water a day is one of the simplest ways to ensure weight loss. A great many overweight people don't drink enough liquid, and misinterpret thirst signs as calls for food. Often, a glass of water will free you from an uncomfortable and difficult-to-resist food craving. Moreover, water helps your body work more efficiently.

• *Increase your daily activity.* In addition to regular exercise, look for ways to put more movement into everyday activities—park the car at the far end of the lot, go for an evening walk with your mate, or take an extra flight of stairs!

Finally, Enjoy Yourself!

By now I hope you realize that going on a diet doesn't have to be a grim affair. It isn't a punishment and you shouldn't look on it as deprivation. True, you are giving up overeating, but without excessive amounts of food cluttering up your life, you'll be free to see and explore things you may have overlooked before. I sometimes liken it to removing dark glasses and seeing the world in all its colors. So be sure to reward yourself as you diet, as we discussed on Days 6 and 9, and give yourself full permission to explore other activities and interests. Laugh, relax, have a good time, enjoy the body that is growing slimmer and healthy each day—after all, you deserve it!

APPENDIX I:
HOW TO
CHOOSE A DIET

ALMOST EVERY magazine, talk show, and book stand boasts a "new" or "revolutionary" weight-loss method. If you're confused about how to lose weight and keep it off, I don't blame you. Many people have been wandering blindly through the diet maze for years. If you've been one of them, now's the time to make yourself an informed consumer. To begin, let's look at the common ways of tackling the problem: through diet, through exercise, through group support, through psychological assistance, and through medical assistance.

Diets

A weight-loss diet is nothing more than a program of eating designed to force the body to burn its reserves of stored fat. Here are some basic diets that you are likely to encounter.

Low-calorie diets

The most familiar diet in America is probably the diet that restricts the individual to 1,000 to 1,800 calories a day depending on sex, age, and overall physical condition. A low-calorie diet that is nutritionally balanced is, in my opinion, the safest and most effective way to lose weight. It can be followed as long as necessary, it poses no side effects or health hazards, and it yields genuine—rather than illusory—results.

Very-low-calorie diets

Very-low-calorie diets—sometimes referred to as crash diets or limited-fast diets—restrict intake to 800 calories or fewer a day. Calories come in the form of food, a special product or formula, or a combination of both. These diets were developed and intended for use *only* by very obese individuals (those weighing twice as much as desirable) and *only* under close medical supervision. Unfortunately, these programs have made their way to the over-the-counter market, where they are frequently used by the wrong people and without the proper medical supervision. No matter how "safe" one of these diets may claim to be, do not consider it unless you are under a physician's care and he or she has recommended it. It is true that several of these diets meet federal RDA (Recommended Daily Allowance) standards, but these standards do not apply to a body in a state of semistarvation. Without supervision, the unmonitored dieter can suffer from several nutritional deficiencies, including mineral and electrolyte losses that may, in extreme cases, lead to cardiac arrest and death. Lesser side effects can include constipation, fatigue, fainting, dry skin, and hair loss. Yet another possible side effect of semistarvation is a slowdown of the body's metabolism, making future weight gain more likely.

Low-fat diets

Since the average American diet is much too high in fat, reducing dietary fat is usually an effective and healthy way of cutting calories. If you choose this method remember that, as with calories, the diet should not be *too* restrictive. Some fat is necessary for good health, and trying to go cold turkey may leave you feeling so deprived you won't be able to follow the diet. Look for a food plan that derives 20 to 30 percent of total caloric intake from fat.

Low-carbohydrate diets

This kind of diet counts carbohydrates, not calories, and seems to achieve prompt and satisfactory results by limiting carbohydrate intake to 100 grams or fewer a day. However, since many healthy fruits and vegetables are high in carbohydrates, the dieter may be tempted to eliminate these foods from his or her menu in order to include refined carbohydrate items like pastry, candy, etc. If you are considering a low-carbohydrate diet, you should be aware that the results are not always as satisfying as they seem because a significant amount of the weight lost is water weight, not fat. For some dieters, nausea and fatigue are also problems. Finally, some studies indicate that overrestriction of carbohydrates promotes food cravings that may lead to binge eating. If you choose a low-carbohydrate diet, look for one that derives about 55 percent of daily caloric intake from the complex carbohydrates in vegetables, fruits, breads, and cereals.

Fad diets

Fad diets usually promote a specific food, product, or theory. Often they claim to make use of "new" and "scientific" principles: that you will not gain weight if you don't eat after a specific time of day, that certain foods eaten in combination will promote slenderness, that food allergies (rather than overeating) make people fat. There is no scientific data to support the food-allergy theory, nor is there evidence (despite bestselling books) that combinations of food or reliance on a particular food will promote weight loss. The only time fad diets work is when they trick you into eating less food than you usually do. Since fad diets are often nutritionally unbalanced, you cannot follow them for any length of time. Even short stints may result in problems like nausea, fatigue, and diarrhea.

Formula diets

Like very-low-calorie diets, formula diets severely limit caloric intake by replacing one, two, or all meals a day with a prepared formula. While such diets can be useful for truly obese patients, they are dangerous unless monitored by a doctor. Self-administered formula diets sold over the counter are no better than fad diets. While such diets do result in rapid weight loss, follow-up studies indicate that, unless the dieter has been helped to modify his or her eating behavior, the weight is regained as soon as the dieter switches back to "real" food.

Exercise

Exercise and diet are complementary halves of a dynamic whole. Neither is likely to be completely satisfactory on its own, but a weight-loss program that pairs diet and exercise is dramatically effective. The most effective form of exercise for burning calories (and strengthening the cardiovascular system) is aerobic exercise—brisk activity that increases your heartbeat for a sustained length of time. Popular forms of aerobic activity include brisk walking, jogging, swimming, cycling, and continuous movement exercise routines set to music. Low-impact aerobic exercises are considered the safest for people of all ages.

Group Support

Group support for weight loss usually pairs a recommended diet plan with counseling and/or regular get-togethers with other dieters. One of the best-known national examples of the group-support method is Weight Watchers. Dieters are weighed in, given a low-fat, low-calorie diet to follow, and invited to participate in group meetings. In addition, Weight Watchers markets a wide variety of low-calorie food items, making the program easy to follow even for those who don't have the time or inclination to cook.

Another national group-support system is Overeaters Anonymous, a not-for-profit concern modeled after (and affiliated with) Alcoholics Anonymous. While OA does offer members a recommended diet plan, the focus is on the psychological aspects of overeating rather than on the scale or the clothing size. OA members look upon their relationship to food as addictive and work toward breaking the cycle of abuse. Telephone numbers for local chapters of both Overeaters Anonymous and Weight Watchers can be found in your local directory.

Psychological Assistance

Psychological assistance can help you in a number of ways. It can provide a source of support as you diet. It can help you gain insight into your problem. It can help you reevaluate your relationship with food. It can help you reshape your eating behavior. Here's what it cannot do: It cannot give you motivation. It cannot wave a magic wand and make you thin. People who expect miracles to happen automatically while in psychoanalysis or any other form of psychotherapy are likely to be disappointed no matter what issue is at hand, and weight loss is no exception. While insight and awareness can be immensely helpful, the most effective approach is one that also makes use of behavior modification.

Behavior modification is exactly what the name implies: a process that changes an individual's habitual behavior. While it might be interesting and helpful to discuss the way your mother forced you to clean your plate as a child, this awareness alone will do nothing to make you slim. You must also learn how to stop cleaning your plate *today*, and that is what effective psychological assistance will aim for.

Psychologists and other psychotherapists trained in behavior modification can be found in virtually every city in America, in private practice, in community mental health facilities, in teaching hospitals, and obesity clinics (see the section on medical assistance, below).

Another helpful form of psychological assistance can be found in hypnotherapy. For the person who has decided to change his or her eating patterns, hypnotherapy can be a useful tool, helping the dieter to become aware of—and able to control—his behavior. However, hypnotherapy is not a magic wand. If you really want to eat pizza, no hypnotherapist can "suggest" otherwise.

Medical Assistance

How do you tell a good doctor from a bad one? First of all, you should know that, just as there are doctors that specialize in gynecology, the skeletal system, and so on, there are doctors that specialize in weight problems. The American Society of Bariatric Physicians can refer you to someone in your area. Their phone number is (303) 779-4833.

When you're evaluating a doctor, look for someone whose manner is both professionally and personally acceptable to you. In addition to having the proper credentials, does the doctor make you feel comfortable and at home? Do you receive adequate time and attention? Can you ask questions freely? Does the doctor encourage you to talk about your eating habits and help you develop new behavior patterns? Can he or she be reached by telephone if it's necessary? Is the doctor's own weight under control? A good doctor should get a "yes" on all of these questions.

A doctor who leaves most of the work to his staff and sees you only for a few brief minutes, whose manner discourages rather than encourages open discussion, is not the right doctor for you. You want to feel that your doctor listens to you, respects you, and treats you like an individual, not just a "case."

What can a doctor do for you? First of all, he can help you with a diet. If you want to lose ten or twenty pounds, you may have little trouble finding a diet and sticking with it for a month or two on your own. But if you have a great deal of weight to lose, you may be facing a year or even more of dieting. A doctor can be especially helpful to you since she can monitor your health and adjust your diet to help you keep losing when you hit a plateau.

A doctor is also necessary if you are considering drugs or surgery as aids in weight loss. Although the majority of doctors no longer prescribe amphetamines for weight loss, a new generation of nonaddictive appetite suppressants has come on the market. Such drugs can help a person at the beginning of a diet or in other short-term situations, and only a doctor can prescribe them. Because these drugs only help to suppress the appetite, they are most effective when combined with a sensible weight-reduction program. There are also several good over-the-counter appetite suppressants. As with any drug, these should be used with caution.

Surgical alternatives have also received a lot of attention in recent years. Stomach stapling works by reducing the size of the stomach and thereby limiting the amount of food the dieter can eat. Internal bypass surgery works by shortening the length of the intestine, thus giving food less of an opportunity to be absorbed. While both of these techniques are effective, they—like very-low-calorie diets—were developed only for extreme cases of obesity. They are not "painless" ways of dieting and will not be performed by reputable doctors unless the patient's immediate health is threatened. Even for patients who are very obese, they are considered treatments of last resort. (Another surgical method, the gastric balloon, has been almost completely abandoned because it is both impractical and laden with troublesome side effects.)

Perhaps the most misunderstood surgical technique available today is liposuction. Many people have the false belief that this is the magic solution they have been waiting for. "You just go under," I overheard one woman tell her friend, "and they vacuum all the fat out." Not quite. Liposuction is not an effective way of dealing with overweight. It's much more a "finishing touch" technique that comes into play *after* someone has reached goal weight. At this time, there may be a few stubborn pounds that the body absolutely refuses to surrender. Usually these pounds are in predictable "fat depots"—the thighs, buttocks, and so forth. This is quite different from general overweight, where fat is distributed throughout the body.

The Right Diet

On pages 211–217 you'll find the diet I give to the patients I handle in private practice. Unless there is a specific reason why you cannot follow this diet (such as a food allergy or a vegetarian lifestyle), I strongly recommend this diet to you. It is low in calories and in fat, it is nutritionally sound, and it will not leave you feeling hungry or deprived.

Will you give my diet a try?

(Your answer) _____

If you answered yes, go right on and become acquainted with my diet.

If you answered no to my question, examine your reasons carefully. If you have already found a diet that will be just as nutritious and effective, go to it! Just be certain that you aren't shopping for a "dream diet" that doesn't exist.

I realize that there are hundreds of diets on the market today and that many of them make tempting claims. "Eat your way thin," trumpets one advertisement. "Lose a pound a day painlessly," promises another. "Dessert can't hurt," claims still another, "as long as you remember to take one little pill . . ."

The truth is that the diet of one's dreams, like a prince on a white horse, usually doesn't exist. There is no magic potion that will allow you to eat to your heart's content (or, more accurately, to your heart's discontent) and still lose weight.

Before choosing any diet or weight-loss method, please make sure your diet complies with the following criteria:

- *It keeps you from getting too hungry.* Surprised? Don't be. A little hunger is to be expected, but when you become *too* hungry a number of destructive things happen. One is that you lose energy, undermining any exercise program you have committed to. You may also become depressed—so depressed that you lose your motivation. A third consequence is that your starving body begins to crave "quick-fix" foods like simple carbohydrates (breads, pastries, sweets, etc.) and this can lead to binge eating. Check the total calorie intake per day of any diet you're considering. If the amount is too low (below 800 to 1000 calories per day for women and 1200 to 1500 calories per day for men), beware. Besides leaving you dangerously hungry and possibly undernourished, such diets may be counterproductive. Research indicates that the resilient, resourceful body will quickly learn to survive at this "starvation" level. In other words, eating dramatically less food doesn't necessarily result in an equally dramatic weight loss. It may actually reduce your body's basal metabolism (baseline energy consumption) permanently, thus making future weight gain much more likely.

- *It includes a variety of foods.* Rice is fine, but man and woman should never live by rice alone. The same goes for pineapple, protein, salad, water, popcorn, and all the other foods that have been transformed into one-item diets. Similarly, diets that restrict you to a single category of foods—such as fruit-only diets or protein-only diets—are also to be avoided. A diet that abolishes whole food groups is probably a diet you won't be able to stay with. Who wants to face a life without bread, for instance? Or pasta? Diets that completely eliminate the very foods you enjoy will only bring out the rebellious streak in you. Moreover, these diets teach you nothing. They imply that you can either feast and be fat or abstain and be thin when they should be teaching you how to eat all foods moderately. Remember, your body needs a variety of foods to get the nutrients it requires, and your soul thrives on variety to keep going. A diet that offers a diversity of textures and tastes will prevent you from becoming bored.

- *It takes off weight at a steady, reasonable pace.* Weight isn't easy to lose, and diets that promise instant success are usually relying on some sort of gimmick. A diet that depletes your fluid resources, for example, may take off ten pounds in a few days. But what you've lost is ten pounds of water, not ten pounds of stored fat. Studies indicate that when weight comes off slowly, the dieter has a much better chance of keeping it off. In the first week of a diet you may be delighted to lose five or even more pounds, but somewhere along the line you'll hit a plateau and your rate will drop to a few pounds a week or even less. A good diet is geared to this sure-but-steady pace.

- *It restricts the amount you eat.* Some tricky diets offer you unlimited amounts of certain foods. I don't think this is a good idea. Such diets, well-meaning though they may be, encourage you to keep overeating. Even though the food you're overeating may be "harmless," the pattern isn't. It's destructive—especially when you go off the diet and go back to foods that are high in fat and sugar. Learning to eat in moderation is important.

- *It encourages healthy eating habits.* Twenty years ago, the low-carbohydrate diet came into fashion with a roar. One of the highly recommended snacks was fried pork rinds—little strips of rind deep-fried, like potato chips, in oil. Since the rinds contain no carbohydrates at all, the dieter was encouraged to slake his hunger on unlimited amounts of this high-calorie, high-fat snack. Does this sound healthy to you? A good diet encourages healthy eating habits like moderation. It should also teach you common, sensible practices, such as removing skin from poultry, trimming fat off meat, eliminating or restricting alcohol consumption, and so on.

- *It's a diet you can stay on for the rest of your life.* This is a simple acid test in evaluating any prospective diet. Ask yourself what would happen if you stayed on it for the rest of your life. Would you become gradually unhealthy and malnourished? Would you feel horribly depressed and deprived? If you can answer these two questions with a no, you have found a good diet.

- *It's flexible and realistic.* Dieting isn't something you do on an isolated mountaintop. Life—with all its distractions and demands—is going to be going on all around you. Be sure your diet takes this into account. A diet that is too rigid—demanding that on Friday at noon you eat buckwheat pasta with pine nuts and *only* buckwheat pasta with pine nuts, for instance—is too dictatorial to follow. Look for a diet that offers alternatives or lets you switch days to accommodate unforeseen changes in your schedule.

• *It takes your current physical state into account.* To be successful, a diet must supply your body with less fuel than it needs, forcing it to burn the fuel it has stored as fat. Not all bodies can lose weight on the same diet. A woman who is postmenopausal, for example, needs dramatically fewer calories than her twenty-year-old daughter and will have to go on a lower calorie diet to lose weight. Whatever diet you choose, make sure it takes such factors into account.

• *It includes a maintenance program.* Dieting is hard. But not as hard as making the transition from dieting to maintenance. This is the crucial point that all too many programs ignore. A good diet will give you guidelines, not only for losing weight but for keeping it off.

• *It meets your lifestyle needs.* If you truly enjoy cooking, look for a diet that offers lots of low-calorie recipes for you to try. If the thought of making food choices every day fills you with anxiety, select a diet that makes all the choices for you in advance. And if you are working with a limited budget, don't opt for the "Caviar and Dom Pérignon Diet." You wouldn't buy a dining room table without deciding how much you had to spend on it or what size it should be to fit nicely into your home, so don't buy a diet that won't fit into your life. For example, if your job necessitates frequent business lunches or dinners, a strict, regimented diet that doesn't allow for flexibility will not be right for you. If you have a lactose intolerance, hypoglycemia, or observe religious restrictions you will need a diet tailor-made to your needs.

Use the space below to write down the things your diet must provide. What I want in a diet:

1. _____

_____

2. _____

_____

3. _____

_____

4. _____

_____

5. _____

_____

6. _____

_____

The DeBetz Diet

On the following pages, you'll find the diet I've created to help hundreds of my patients lose weight. But first, I've provided some important guidelines that you will need to know in order to get the most out of your dieting experience.

Guidelines for the DeBetz Diet

I've designed this diet to be as easy to follow as possible. Just keep these simple guidelines in mind when you use it.

- *Follow the daily diet listings every day.* Don't make substitutions and don't deviate. If you're dining at a restaurant, choose foods from the menu that are in accord with the diet.

- *Eat moderate portions only.* One of the wonderful things about this diet, patients tell me, is not having to count calories or portion food. I've done that work for you in advance. If you follow the diet and eat moderate portions where indicated, you will be losing weight on 900 to 1200 calories per day. In general, a moderate portion of chicken or fish is about six ounces, most meat portions are about four ounces, vegetables one cup, and cereals one cup.

- *Don't drink any high-calorie beverages.* The beverages in the diet are meant to be water, mineral water, coffee, tea, or sugar-free soda, all preferably low-sodium.

- *Don't use fats in cooking, food preparation, or as additives.* "One slice toast" means toast without butter or margarine, which has the same caloric content as butter. You may use nonstick vegetable sprays in cooking, and lemon juice, vinegar, or low-calorie dressing as seasoning on salads. But no oils, please!

- *Remove skin and all visible fat from any servings.* Select lean meats only and always trim cuts of visible fats. Be sure to remove the skin from poultry, and other meats as it is very high in calories.

- *Eat plenty of vegetables.* Fresh vegetables, high in vitamins and minerals, should be part of every lunch and dinner. Flavor them with lemon juice, vinegar, or low-calorie dressings—not butter, margarine, oil, or sauces. Fruits are to be eaten only according to daily listings. No sugar or syrups are to be added.

- *Between meals, use the Stoplines as often as needed.* Using the Stoplines will keep you from breaking your diet with high-calorie snacks.

- *Enjoy low-calorie snacks between meals.* If you are hungry between meals, snack on low-sodium consommé and broth (fewer than 13 calories per cup, spiced with herbs and seasonings, if desired), raw vegetables (spiced with lemon juice, vinegar, and seasonings), and sugar-free gelatin desserts (several times a day, if you wish).

- *Don't take drugs or use "reducing devices" without your doctor's approval.* Don't take chances on "miracle" drugs that promise to help you lose weight painlessly—all you'll lose is your money and your motivation. Although my diet is nutritionally balanced to provide for your body's basic needs, you may take a daily vitamin-mineral capsule if you like.

• *Remember that you don't have to eat everything on your plate.* If you feel full or want to skip something on the list for one reason or another, go right ahead. Learn to recognize your body's fullness signals! If you like, save your uneaten food to snack on when you are hungry.

Repeat the DeBetz Diet every week until you've lost the desired weight or create your own variations by interchanging proteins, vegetables, and fruit.

DAY 1

BREAKFAST

1 small banana or ½ large banana, sliced or other style
½ cup unsugared dry or hot cereal with
4 ounces skim milk
Beverage

LUNCH

3 ounces salad of tuna or salmon (water-packed, low-sodium preferably; if tuna is in oil, wash it in a sieve under running water and pat dry with paper towels), plain or with lemon juice, vinegar, low-calorie salad dressing (no more than 16 calories per tablespoon, and no more than 1 tablespoon), or 1 teaspoon of low-calorie imitation mayonnaise.
Lettuce, carrots, cherry tomatoes, cucumber, celery
2 low-calorie crackers (melba toast, wafers, crisps, etc.)
Beverage

DINNER

1 consommé (preferably low-sodium)
1 moderate slice roast lamb or veal
Cauliflower or brussels sprouts, cooked zucchini and onions
Salad of lettuce, radishes, green peppers, and tomatoes
½ cup sugar-free applesauce
Beverage

DAY 2

BREAKFAST

1 medium orange, sliced or sectioned
½ cup low-fat cottage cheese
1 slice whole-wheat toast
Beverage

LUNCH

Hot vegetable plate: spinach, broiled tomato, summer squash, mushrooms, green
    beans
2 pieces low-calorie melba toast
½ grapefruit
Beverage

Alternate lunch: You may substitute Day 2's lunch for any other day's with
    vegetables of your choice having the same calories.

DINNER

6 ounces red snapper, flounder, fillet of sole, or other lean fish
Asparagus spears, broccoli
Salad of watercress, cherry tomatoes, cucumbers
½ cantaloupe or 1 melon slice
Beverage

DAY 3

BREAKFAST

1 small or ½ large baked apple, no sugar added
1 poached egg on
1 slice whole-wheat toast
Beverage

LUNCH

1 moderate slice turkey, all skin and visible fat removed
Salad of lettuce, tomato wedges, shredded cabbage (as coleslaw, if desired, with
    seasonings, lemon juice, vinegar or low-calorie salad dressing)
Beverage

DINNER

1 cup beef bouillon
4 ounces broiled lean hamburger steak
Broiled tomato, summer squash
Salad of endive, celery, cucumbers
Sugar-free gelatin dessert
Beverage

DAY 4

BREAKFAST

3 ounces crushed pineapple in natural juice, no sugar added
½ cup unsugared dry or hot cereal with
4 ounces skim milk
Beverage

LUNCH

Fruit salad plate: apple slices, grapefruit segments, sliced half pear or small
    bunch of grapes, lettuce, topped with
3 ounces low-fat cottage cheese
2 low-calorie flatbread wafers
Beverage

DINNER

1 cup fat-free chicken broth (preferably low-sodium)
6 ounces chicken (skin and all visible fat removed)
Green beans, spinach
Salad of lettuce, onion, radishes
½ grapefruit, segmented if preferred
Beverage

DAY 5

BREAKFAST

½ grapefruit (use half remaining from the night before)
½ cup unsugared dry or hot cereal with
4 ounces skim milk
Beverage

LUNCH

½ cantaloupe or 1 honeydew wedge
1 cup vegetable soup or clam chowder (no milk or cream), fat-free, low-salt
2 low-calorie bran wafers or 1 rice cracker
Sugar-free gelatin dessert
Beverage

DINNER

1 cup clam broth or consommé (preferably low-sodium)
6 ounces broiled scallops or halibut steak
1 small boiled potato, cooked carrots or small boiled onions
Salad of raw spinach with low-calorie dressing
1 orange, sliced
Beverage

DAY 6

BREAKFAST

½ cantaloupe or 6 strawberries
1 egg, boiled, poached, fried, or scrambled without fat (use nonstick vegetable
    spray, if desired)
1 slice whole-wheat toast, with sugar-free fruit spread, if desired
Beverage

LUNCH

1 cup broth (preferably low-sodium)
3 ounces chicken salad made with low-calorie imitation mayonnaise and
    chopped celery, a few capers, diced green pepper, served on lettuce with
    carrot and cucumber spears or snow peas
2 pieces melba toast
Beverage

DINNER

4 ounces salt-free tomato juice (you may add herbs, spices)
Broiled steak or 1 slice roast beef, lamb, or veal (all visible fat removed)
Asparagus spears, broiled mushrooms
Salad of endive (or lettuce) with green peppers, cherry tomatoes, chives
½ baked apple, no sugar added
Beverage

DAY 7

BREAKFAST

½ grapefruit or fresh fruit cup
⅔ cup cooked unsugared oatmeal or farina or dry cereal with
4 ounces skim milk
Beverage

LUNCH

6 ounces cold fillet of sole or other fish, or shrimp or other shellfish (plain or as salad)
Lettuce or endive, tomato wedges, cold cooked green beans, olives, radishes, red pepper strips
2 low-calorie breadsticks
Beverage

DINNER

4 ounces vegetable juice, low-sodium
6 ounces chicken (broiled, roasted, poached, or barbecued)
Stewed tomatoes, zucchini, combined with eggplant
Salad of mixed greens
Sugar-free gelatin dessert
Beverage

Creating Your Own Diet

Yes, you can create your own diet—one completely geared to your lifestyle and tastes. Many of you are used to diets that tell you when to eat, what to eat, and how to eat it. While some people find such strict guidelines helpful, others just want to rebel against them. Have you ever created your own diet? You may just discover that giving this control to yourself makes you much more willing to comply.

In creating your own diet, I urge you to be imaginative. Include plenty of different flavors and textures to keep yourself interested and satisfied. If you hate carrot sticks, don't include them just because they're low-calorie—you'll only end up skipping them, and this will leave you with an empty spot in your stomach. Instead, look for a low-calorie alternative that appeals to you—a few fresh strawberries, for example, or green pepper rings.

All I ask is that you follow the guidelines for a good diet listed earlier in this appendix and keep your diet low in fat and calories. If you don't know the nutritional content of foods, buy yourself an inexpensive reference guide.

Below you'll find blank spaces for creating lists of the good, healthy, low-calorie foods you wish to include in your diet. Enjoy yourself!

Foods I Like that Are *Very* Low in Calories

_____	_____	_____
_____	_____	_____
_____	_____	_____
_____	_____	_____
_____	_____	_____
_____	_____	_____
_____	_____	_____

Foods I Like that Are *Moderately* Low in Calories

_____	_____	_____
_____	_____	_____
_____	_____	_____
_____	_____	_____
_____	_____	_____
_____	_____	_____
_____	_____	_____

Foods I Like that Are *Higher* in Calories
but Healthful and Extremely Satisfying to Me

_____	_____	_____
_____	_____	_____
_____	_____	_____
_____	_____	_____
_____	_____	_____
_____	_____	_____

APPENDIX II:
DESIRABLE
WEIGHT CHARTS

WOMEN

Height	Small Frame	WEIGHT IN POUNDS Medium Frame	Large Frame
4'10"	102–111	109–121	118–131
4'11"	103–113	111–123	120–134
5'0"	104–115	113–126	122–137
5'1"	106–118	115–129	125–140
5'2"	108–121	118–132	128–143
5'3"	111–124	121–135	131–147
5'4"	114–127	124–138	134–151
5'5"	117–130	127–141	137–155
5'6"	120–133	130–144	140–159
5'7"	123–136	133–147	143–163
5'8"	126–139	136–150	146–167
5'9"	129–142	139–153	149–170
5'10"	132–145	142–156	152–173
5'11"	135–148	145–159	155–176
6'0"	138–151	148–162	158–179

Source: Metropolitan Life Height and Weight Tables. Courtesy of Metropolitan Life Insurance Company.

MEN

Height	WEIGHT IN POUNDS		
	Small Frame	Medium Frame	Large Frame
5′2″	128–134	131–141	138–150
5′3″	130–136	133–143	140–153
5′4″	132–138	135–145	142–156
5′5″	134–140	137–148	144–160
5′6″	136–142	139–151	146–164
5′7″	138–145	142–154	149–168
5′8″	140–148	145–157	152–172
5′9″	142–151	148–160	155–176
5′10″	144–154	151–163	158–180
5′11″	146–157	154–166	161–184
6′0″	149–160	157–170	164–188
6′1″	152–164	160–174	168–192
6′2″	155–168	164–178	172–197
6′3″	158–172	167–182	176–202
6′4″	162–176	171–187	181–207

APPENDIX III:
Rx FOR "CRISIS MOTIVATION"

WHY DO so many people fail to lose weight or keep it off? Below are some of the common motivational crises people have asked me about—and prescriptions for overcoming them.

CRISIS: Last year I lost a good deal of weight to be in my sister's wedding. I looked and felt great, but the minute the wedding was over, I started to gain the weight back. What can I do?

Rx: You know how to diet; it's just a question of finding a goal that will motivate you. Your sister's wedding was an effective incentive, but when it was over your goal vanished. To lose the weight you've regained you need to set a new goal, one that won't go away. It can be your enjoyment of a *permanently* slim body, a lifetime of good health, a greater choice in the clothes you wear—whatever has particular meaning for you. (See the sections on setting goals and rewards on pages 110–114.) Then use self-hypnosis (pages 97–101) and visualization (pages 114–115) to focus on your goal several times each day as you bring your eating under control once more.

CRISIS: I want to lose weight, but my "food connection" goes all the way back to childhood. My mother always made us clean our plates, telling us there were starving children all over the world. Now that I'm grown up, my husband expects me to cook a big, delicious dinner every night. With all that food around, no wonder I can't resist!

Rx: You're doing something a lot of overweight people do: transferring blame. It isn't your mother's fault, your husband's fault, or food's fault that you've gained weight. Your motivation is shaky because you've never accepted responsibility for your eating patterns. Each time you use the Stoplines (page 61) and Supportlines (page 133) pay special attention to the word "I," focusing on the fact that you and you alone are responsible for feeding your body.

CRISIS: Controlling my eating is no problem at all when things are going well in my life. But the minute a crisis arises at work or at home, I find myself overeating. By the time I realize what I'm doing, it's too late—the food's already in my system.

Rx: I won't try to tell you that food isn't soothing. For you, it obviously is, at least temporarily. The problem is that you haven't discovered an alternative to overeating—one that will provide the same comfort without the added calories. You can overcome this destructive eating habit with a number of different techniques: relaxing with self-hypnosis (pages 97–101), soothing yourself with nonfood rewards (pages 165–174), and learning to use the Touch-Control Method (page 61) and the Supportlines (page 133) to avoid eating on impulse.

CRISIS: I can't keep from nibbling food whenever I'm in the kitchen. Please don't tell me to stay out of the kitchen because, as the mother of three children, I have to prepare three meals a day. There's no way I can avoid being around food, and that's the whole problem.

Rx: There are several ways you can overcome the hazardous effects of nibbling. First, you can interrupt your cooking to practice the Touch-Control Method (page 61). Or you can try imagining that the food you're handling is something else: currency, fabric, or clothing. Just as you would not take more than your share of these commodities, so you can remind yourself not to take more than your share of food. If you still cannot keep from nibbling, minimize the damage by *planning* what you will nibble on. You may want to eat your dinner salad or piece of fruit as you cook, and this will allow you to stay on your diet.

CRISIS: My job requires me to entertain clients, and this usually means eating and drinking in high style. No matter how good my intentions are, I find myself tempted by the menu and by the fact that everyone around me is eating a lot. How can I keep up my resolve?

Rx: First, you might look for other ways of entertaining your clients— such as the theater, concerts, or other noneating events. Or you might try switching your appointment to a relaxing late afternoon tea rather than a heavy meal. If you cannot avoid dining with your clients, decide what to have *before* you enter the restaurant. Order a salad (or whatever will fit with your diet that day) without looking at the menu, or ask the waiter to put only half the usual serving size on your plate. If you are having a hard time during the meal, remember that you can practice the Touch-Control Method (page 61) without drawing attention to yourself in any way.

CRISIS: Our family holds a big picnic every Fourth of July, and this year I'd like to attend without blowing my diet. How can I turn down all that potato salad and barbecued ribs?

Rx: First of all, you don't have to turn everything down. Work out in advance what you'll eat and in what amounts. As the event draws near, use visualization (pages 114–115) to see yourself at the picnic. Imagine the event in detail: who will be there, what you'll wear, the good time you'll have. Create a clear image of yourself eating just what you've planned to eat and no more. Envision dialogues in which you say, "Thank you, that was delicious, but I'm not going to have any more." This kind of behavior rehearsal will prepare you to meet the day without succumbing to temptation.

CRISIS: It's not my imagination—my husband really *is* sabotaging my diet. He says he wants me to lose weight but the minute I get serious about a diet, he starts bringing candy bars home from work. If I don't have his support, how can I ever stick to a diet?

Rx: First of all, *your* support is what's important, not your husband's. He may not be helping you, but that doesn't mean you can't stick with your diet. The first thing you have to do is decide to stay with your commitment in spite of the actions and hidden agendas of those around you. How do you do that? Chances are his actions make you angry, and this anger leads you right back to the refrigerator. Instead of "stuffing down" your emotions with food, use self-hypnosis (pages 97–101) to release your anger and focus on your goal of losing weight. Once you've calmed down, you might want to confront your husband directly about what he's doing. If he's unaware of his actions and motives, talking things out may help. (Many husbands secretly fear that a slim, attractive wife will leave them.) If your husband is oblivious to self-examination, see if he'll agree to a few simple rules, like "Don't bring candy home," or "Don't eat 'temptation foods' in front of me."

CRISIS: If I slip up and go off my diet, I figure I've blown it for the day and compound the error by going on a full-scale binge. How can I keep from slipping up?

Rx: You can't. People aren't perfect and everyone will give in to temptation from time to time. The trick is not to let one little slip lead to a major diet setback. My guess is that when you cheat, something like this happens: You tell yourself you're bad, weak-willed, and incapable of sticking to a diet. This kind of thinking leaves you feeling guilty and hopeless, so why not eat? When you slip on a diet, the first thing you need to do is *forgive yourself.* See the incident as a mistake, not a trend. Then reaffirm your commitment to lose weight and go right back on your diet. Rereading "The Power of Self-Talk" and "Changing Negative to Positive" (pages 151–162) should help you overcome your defeatist thinking.

CRISIS: I'm motivated as long as the scale is moving down, but when I hit a plateau and stop losing weight for a few days, I go into a major slump. What's the use of depriving myself if I'm going to stay fat?

Rx: First of all, if you really stay with your diet you *won't* stay fat. Plateaus are a common part of dieting, as the body doesn't always lose weight at a steady pace. The slump you go into suggests that you put too much emphasis on your scale. Stay off it for awhile. Instead of weighing yourself every day, weigh yourself once a week or even once a month. In the meantime, focus on other positive aspects of your diet regime instead: how good it feels to be in control of your eating, or the fact that your clothes fit better.

CRISIS: I have a lot of weight to lose, nearly a hundred pounds. I start a diet, lose ten or twenty pounds easily, and am euphoric. In fact, I'm so pleased with my success that I celebrate by eating—and gaining back several of the pounds I've just lost.

Rx: I don't need to tell you that you're setting a very bad pattern for yourself. First of all, it's hard on the body to keep gaining and losing weight, so begin by focusing on the *attention* and *protection* you owe your body (see the Stoplines, page 61). You're also setting a bad psychological pattern for yourself in that you're still using food as a reward. Work through "Your Personal Prize Package" (pages 110–114) and the several sections in Day 9 that deal with goals and rewards to develop healthier alternatives. Finally, remind yourself that your long-term goal isn't to lose ten or twenty pounds but a hundred, and keep this image firmly in mind. (The "televisualization" technique on page 127 is an especially good way to do this.)

CRISIS: The first week of a diet is always great, the second week possible, the third week difficult, and the fourth impossible. After so many days of deprivation, I just can't face another diet meal. You know how they always say "listen to your body"? Well, my body is screaming for pizza, pasta, and ice cream!

Rx: The problem may be the diet you've chosen. Is it too restrictive? Too repetitive? A diet that deprives you too much and recycles the same foods over and over is not a diet most people can stick with. Check to see that you haven't fallen into a dieting rut. Refer to the list of foods you developed on pages 218–219 in Appendix I to see which items you can integrate into your diet program. If there's a food item you're craving—pizza, for example—go ahead and have it, working it into your diet and arranging your other meals accordingly. Just don't have it on the sly. If these measures don't help, your problem may not be in your mouth or stomach but in your head. Boost your awareness by re-reading "Is It Hunger or Is It Appetite?" (pages 131–134) and the sections on resistance (pages 70–87).

CRISIS: I do well all day at work, eating almost nothing and even skipping lunch without feeling particularly hungry. But the minute I get home I go completely out of control. I live alone, so instead of eating a balanced meal I often snack through the entire evening. Help!—I'm disgusted with myself but I can't seem to break the pattern.

Rx: I see lots of clues to your problem in your question. First, you say you eat "almost nothing" during the day and "even" skip lunch. This isn't a good idea. You're letting yourself get far too hungry. Work keeps you busy and distracted but the minute you get home, those hunger pangs come roaring to life. Many overweight people save up meals so that they can have one big binge—a destructive way to feed yourself. Don't skip lunch but eat a moderate, healthful meal. If you still find yourself overly hungry at dinnertime, you might want to have a late afternoon snack—like a piece of fruit or some yogurt. Taking the edge off your hunger will allow you to prepare a sensible, moderate evening meal. Try scheduling a few quiet moments on your way home from work or as soon as you walk in the door to reaffirm your motivation with the Stoplines (page 61), Supportlines (page 133), and self-hypnosis (pages 97–101). Another problem may be that you're using food to fill up your evenings. In this case, the work you did on Day 9 (particularly the sections on "Learning to Do" and "Learning to Feel Good Without Food" on pages 176–178) should help you out.

INDEX

About the Author

BARBARA DeBETZ, M.D., is a psychiatrist and a bariatrician, a specialist in matters of weight control. Dr. DeBetz has developed her weight-control program over seventeen years of practice in New York City. She is Assistant Clinical Professor of Psychiatry at Columbia University College of Physicians and Surgeons.